OWN YOUR CULTURE

HOW TO DEFINE, EMBED AND MANAGE YOUR COMPANY CULTURE

BRETTON PUTTER

CultureGene

For Monica, Yuna and Rafa

About the author

Bretton Putter is the founder and CEO of CultureGene, a company culture leadership platform, which enables leaders to build a strong, functional company culture. Prior to founding CultureGene Brett spent 16 years as the Managing Partner of a leading executive search firm based in London working with startups and high-growth companies in the UK, Europe and USA. Brett published his first book *Culture Decks Decoded* in 2018.

Thanks

Thanks to the leaders who offered up their time to share their experiences and knowledge to help make this book happen.

Tom Bogan, CEO, Adaptive Insights

Rikke Rosenlund, CEO, BorrowMyDoggy

Dame Stephanie Shirley, CEO, Freelance Programmers

Mark Organ, Chairman, Influitive

Bernhard Niesner, CEO, busuu

David Cummings, CEO, Pardot & Atlanta Ventures

Kyle Porter, CEO, SalesLoft

Christine Kaszubski, Chief People Officer, SalesLoft

Rob O'Donovan, Chairman, CharlieHR

Alicia Navarro, CEO, Skimlinks

Kieran O'Neill, CEO, Thread

Amanda Lannert, CEO, Jellyvision

Joel Montgomery, VP of Culture, CloudFactory

David Darmanin, CEO, Hotjar

Gerald Kullack, CEO, Lillydoo

Bronwen Loubser, CEO, Frames@53

Adam Posma, Chairman, ClubCollect

Stan McCleod, CEO, Headliner

Ohad Hecht, CEO, Emarsys

Robert Williams, CEO, PlumbGuarantee

Sanjay Singhal, CEO, Audiobooks

Paddy Moogan, cofounder, Aira

Colette Ballou, CEO, Ballou

Natasha Guerra, CEO, Runway East

Rick Perrault, CEO, Unbounce

Melanie Tantingco, VP People Operations, Periscope Data

Andreas Klinger, Head of Remote, AngelList

Maarten Roerink, former CEO, Guidion

Mihai Bocai, CEO, Evonomix

Melissa Andrada, COO, Learnerbly

Anneka Gupta, President, LiveRamp
Nicolas Dessaigne, former CEO, Algolia
Tushar Agarwal, CEO, HubbleHQ
Tom Watson, CTO, HubbleHQ
Tamara Littleton, CEO, The Social Element
Franz-Joseph Miller, CEO, time:matters
Travis Terrell, co-CEO, Soundstripe
Paul Archer, CEO, Duel
Neal Vance, CEO, NI
Nic Brisbourne, Managing Partner, Forward Partners
Becky Gooch & Graham Laming, Next Jump
Tarun Gidoomal & Kevin McCoy, Next Jump
Nick Black, President, CloudMade
Evgeny Shadchnev, CEO, Makers
Karen Holden, Managing Director, A City Law Firm
Daniel Reilly, CEO, Ruler Analytics
Antonio Cantalapiedra Asensio, CEO, Spain & Portugal, MyTaxi
David Jackson, Business Development Manager, Winnow
Frank Johnson, Director, Allied
Vishnu Teja, CEO, AssetVault
Adam Bird, CEO, Cronofy
Misha Gopaul, CEO, FATMAP

Thanks to Nic Brisbourne for writing the foreword to this book.

For me, writing a book is like walking through waste-high mud in waders, while wrestling a giant anaconda. I recommend these fabulous people who all played an essential role in getting my writing into a readable form. Thanks to Adam Martin, Brian Baker, Elloa Phoenix Barbour, Angela Panayotopulo, Cheryl Lenser and David Prendergast.

Extra, extra special thanks to my wife Monica without whom this book would never have been written.

Praise for *Own Your Culture*

"Culture is priority #1. No one captures it better than Bretton Putter"

David Cummings, Founder Atlanta Ventures

Own Your Culture delivers a framework and sorely needed model for how you can build your own version of amazing. I found my head nodding with each page I turned "yup, yes, yup, uh-huh, yes…" constantly. This should be required reading for every leader who aspires to achieve success today in their organization. You need to read Bretton Putter's book."

Steve Cadigan, former VP Talent LinkedIn, Founder Cadigan Talent Ventures

"Brett does a beautiful job of providing tangible actions for leaders to bring to life the intangible nature of culture."

Padma Thiruvengadam, former Chief People Officer LEGO, CHRO Takeda Pharmaceuticals

"*Own Your Culture* will help you develop a strong culture and future-proof your business."

Paul Nixon, CEO LGTVestra US

"The timing for this book could not be better. Every business leader who wants to develop and strengthen the glue that is their organization's culture should read this book."

Nora Rothrock, CEO US Tax and Financial

"This book is powerful and so crucial, especially given all that is happening in the business world right now."

Romanie Thomas, CEO JuggleJobs

"This book is packed with actionable ideas, tools, techniques, and real-life stories that will help you design and develop the culture you want for your business."

Simone Maini, COO Elliptic

"Culture defines how a company hires, engages customers, builds product, partners with other companies, and ultimately treats all shareholders. *Own Your Culture* is the starting block to help you on the journey of crafting your company's culture."

Carlos Espinal, Partner SeedCamp

"*Own Your Culture* is the first book that truly demystifies how startups and high-growth companies develop such powerful company cultures."

Ed Spiegel, CEO Peer Medical

"There is no longer any excuse. Everyone can build a great company culture using the tools and techniques in this book."

Ivailo Jordanov, Partner 7% Ventures

"*Own Your Culture* will help you build a culture to inspire your people and enable them to do their best work."

Bronwen Loubser, CEO Frames@53

"Read this book if you would like to build, improve, or simply learn about the importance of company culture."

Yury Tereshchenko, Director Evori

Table of Contents

Foreword

It is widely recognized that developing and managing culture is a core competence for successful businesses. That's why I'm a big fan of this book and have a deep interest in company culture and the work that Brett is doing.

I believe that we are on the cusp of a new era. An era in which businesses acting in their own self-interest deliver society from what many now describe as "The Meaning Crisis." Whether we enter that era is up to us. To seize the opportunity will be challenging, but if we are successful, the reward will be substantial.

The Meaning Crisis is a term coined by John Vervaeke, a Professor of Psychology and Philosophy at Toronto University, to explain that many of society's problems stem from the fact that over the last thousand years or so, meaning has been slowly stripped from our lives. We feel less connected to our families and institutions, which is the root cause of a range of ills, from the mental health crisis to widespread dissatisfaction at work and with our political leaders. Most of all, we can see the meaning crisis in the results of survey after survey, which show that despite the fact we are wealthier, healthier and safer than ever before, we are no happier. We also know that when people report feeling meaning in their lives there is a strong correlation with feelings of happiness.

Recent work by Vervaeke and others has established the three components of meaning:

- Coherence - when you understand your world
- Significance - when you are important in your world
- Purpose - when you are making progress towards an important goal

Most of us can look back fondly on times in our lives when all three components were present. Maybe it was a time when we were falling in love. Our understanding of ourselves and our partner was exploding and seemed almost complete. Our importance to each other was off the charts and progress toward a life of happiness together was rapid. Or maybe it was when we were on a sports or work team that was crushing it. Coherence was off the charts because we knew we had cracked the code. Significance was high because we all knew our roles and how they were critical to team success. Our purpose was winning, and winning we were. These were times when life was rich in meaning.

We've seen over the last 30 years that some businesses have started to harness culture as a business asset. It's now widely understood that intentionally building shared values and approaches to work can yield improved productivity and employee loyalty. Less common, but more impactful is how some visionary leaders are now harnessing corporate culture to create meaning for employees. Companies are doing this in two ways.

The extrinsic approach to corporate meaning-making and most common way is to align their culture around a mission to positively impact the world. Patagonia is perhaps the best known example. They started in 1973, building products for rock climbers that were high quality and cared for the environment. They built a highly authentic brand, which appealed to the climbing community both as employees and as customers. Forty-seven years later their mission statement reads "Build the best product, cause no unnecessary harm, use business to inspire and implement solutions to the environmental crisis"—a mission they are using to create meaning for their employees consistently. Coherence comes from their worldview, which aligns business objectives with the environment. Significance comes from the over $100 million they have donated to preservation and restoration of the natural environment and the thousands of young activists they have trained. Purpose comes from the progress they are making as a company.

The newer intrinsic approach to corporate meaning-making is where companies create meaning for their employees as individuals. It's a much less widely practiced approach, but no less powerful. Next

Jump, one of the companies that Brett talks about in this book, is my favorite example. They have made the personal growth of their employees core to their mission as a business. Everybody at Next Jump is expected to work on themselves every day and they have built a range of rituals and processes such that everyone gets literally hundreds of pieces of feedback every week. Thus they learn about themselves and grow with great rapidity in ways that help not only at work but also at home. This learning gives coherence by improving their understanding of themselves and through that of the world. Significance comes from working at a company and with colleagues that care deeply for their welfare. Purpose comes from the progress they make as individuals and from Next Jump's commercial success.

What is genuinely exciting is the potential of marrying these two approaches. The extrinsic approach to meaning-making provides the ethical dimension that we need to inspire us. The intrinsic approach provides the rituals and daily practices we need to flourish and grow as individuals. Together they offer a potential for widespread meaning-making on a massive scale.

Perhaps what's most important is that we build awareness amongst business leaders and employees that the absence of meaning is a pervasive problem locally and globally, and that we, as individuals, can do something about it. As business leaders, we can build a company culture that creates meaning for our people, both intrinsic and extrinsic, and know that our companies will be stronger if we do. As employees we can seek out the companies that are developing cultures that create meaning for us and know that our lives will be richer as a result.

Own Your Culture is *the* blueprint for building a company culture of meaning and success.

Nic Brisbourne, Managing Partner, Forward Partners

Introduction

The Way We Do Things Around Here

What is company culture? Culture develops in a company when decisions that are made prove to be successful and the thinking that went into those decisions becomes embedded into **the way we do things around here.** Culture is complex. It is invisible, subconscious, intangible, and happens 'below the surface'. The leaders of most organizations don't even know what company culture is, let alone how to develop it into a business asset. Ben Horowitz, cofounder and general partner at Andreessen Horowitz, describes his situation as a first-time CEO:

> "When I first founded a company, one called LoudCloud, I sought advice from CEOs and industry leaders. They all told me, 'Pay attention to your culture. Culture is the most important thing.' But when I asked these leaders, 'What exactly is culture and how can I affect mine?' they became extremely vague. I spent the next eighteen years trying to figure this question out."
> *What You Do Is Who You Are: How to Create Your Business Culture*

A strong, functional culture is the missing link in most businesses, and there are countless leaders in similar situations to Horowitz at LoudCloud. They understand that company culture is essential but don't know what to do about it. With this book I hope to shine a light inside the black box of company culture and give you the tools to develop yours into a visible, conscious, and tangible asset for your organization.

Own Your Culture is the collective wisdom of 50+ leaders I have interviewed over the past three years. Some of the business leaders I have spoken with for this book include:

- Anneka Gupta, President of LiveRamp, who has helped scale the company from a team of 25 when she joined to 1000 people in under 10 years.
- David Cummings who boot-strapped and sold Pardot to Salesforce for $100m, cofounded SalesLoft, Terminus and Atlanta Ventures and was the first investor in Calendly.
- Tom Bogan, CEO of Adaptive Insights, who joined the company when it was generating $40m in revenues and sold it to Workday for $1.5 billion in 2018.
- Dame Stephanie Shirley, founder and CEO of Freelance Programmers, the first 'remote work' company, which at its peak employed 6000 people and had a market capitalization of $1.5 billion.

These culture-driven leaders believe that culture is a vital driving force of their company, in everything they do.

In the chapters ahead you will find examples of what these and other leaders have done and continue to do to make their cultures more visible, conscious, and tangible. From Unbounce's values recognition card game, to Influitive's company-wide nine-minute daily stand-ups, to Hotjar sending new joiners a company credit card once they've signed the employment agreement, to Audiobooks's use of NPS scores as part of the employee probation period.

I begin, in **Chapters 1 to 3**, by focusing on why culture matters, what it is, how a strong, functional culture can impact your company, and why you should start to understand and define your culture as soon as possible.

In **Chapters 4 to 6**, I look at how culture-driven leaders create an environment where their culture can be embodied and "lived," starting from before a candidate applies for a job, through the hiring, onboarding, and employee review processes. I explain how a new employee should be selected for their fit with the values of their company and why trying to hire for "culture fit" is impossible.

Chapter 7 explores what you should do when you hire someone who doesn't fit with your values. **Chapter 8** looks at how to embed culture, while **Chapters 9 and 10** look at techniques that culture-driven leaders use to develop a better and more open workplace by using feedback, developing trust, instilling transparency and using proactive learning for personal and professional improvement.

In **Chapter 11**, I look at the case for Diversity and Inclusion, **Chapters 12 and 13** delve into how leaders build culture for remote, hybrid and distributed office environments and in **Chapter 14** I summarize the key takeaways I have learned researching and conducting the interviews that enabled me to write this book.

In the **Afterword** I look toward the future and explore what culture-driven leadership could evolve into.

My aim with *Own Your Culture* is precisely that, for you to take ownership of your company's culture. What this requires, whether you are building a remote, hybrid or office-based culture, is that you understand:

1. The critical significance of company culture as the one sustainable competitive advantage that you have complete control over.
2. That company culture can be defined, embedded, reinforced and managed in the same way that you manage the other critical functions of your business.

This book will give you the tools and a clear pathway to developing and maintaining a strong, functional company culture: your first step toward becoming a culture-driven leader.

Chapter 1

Why Culture Matters
(Way More Than You Think)

"Culture is the only sustainable competitive advantage
that is completely within the control of the entrepreneur."
– David Cummings, CEO, Pardot & Atlanta Ventures

THE CULTURE-DRIVEN ADVANTAGE

In my last book, *Culture Decks Decoded*, I discussed the light-bulb moment I had about culture-driven leadership. I realized that culture was the missing piece of the puzzle. When the light flashed on in my head, it felt like I had been catapulted into a future where leaders make business decisions based on how those decisions fit and support their living culture. That future, I sensed, would be realized through culture-driven leadership, where business decisions would be made based on how they fit with the company's values, mission and vision.

At that point in my life, I had spent 14 years as the Managing Partner of an executive search firm specializing in working with early-stage high-growth technology companies in the UK, Europe, and the USA. Reflecting on the 400+ executive searches and 5,000+ interviews I had completed, I realized that the CEOs who had a solid understanding of their company's culture had the best outcomes. Those search processes ran a lot more smoothly and they were able to hire the strongest candidates. I also realized that company culture was often the primary reason why a candidate joined a company—a reason that reigned above the salary, stock options or the inherent risk associated

1

with the business. This culture-driven advantage has also been apparent at Seedcamp, where I am one of the founding Limited Partners. I've seen the portfolio companies that have been able to scale successfully—companies like Transferwise (the global money transfer business that's raised $772 million in venture funding and grown to 1,500 employees in nine years) have all had founding CEOs who had a clear understanding, early on, of how crucial their company's culture was to its growth and scale. I also realized that culture is the missing piece of the puzzle for most businesses, not just startups or venture-backed businesses.

This led me to launch CultureGene, a venture focused on helping startups and high-growth companies prepare for and deal with rapid growth challenges. Through the CultureGene Culture Leadership Platform, a software-driven consultancy business, we deliver a three-stage process to help leaders of these companies *define, embed and manage* their culture. The outcome of the Culture Development Process is a well-defined company culture that's understood by employees and deeply embedded into the organization's functions and processes.

As experienced by the CEOs and business leaders I interviewed for this book, the outcomes of a strong, functional company culture include:

- **An understanding of the culture:** Where the values, mission and vision are clearly understood, defined, embedded, reinforced and managed across all business functions and are demonstrably lived by the team every day.
- **Magnetic work environments:** Where the right A+ candidates automatically self-select into the recruitment process and the wrong candidates self-select out.
- **Values-based interview process:** Where a data-driven interview process results in hires being made based on how people's values fit with the organization, NOT how they fit with the culture. I delve deeper into this later in the book.
- **Employee retention:** Where people can self-actualize and are therefore less inclined to want to leave—and you won't want to let them go—because they believe they can fulfill their potential.
- **Management through the values lens:** Where leadership and employees use a values-based, culture-driven framework to make the right decisions for the business;

sometimes to the short-term detriment of the business.

- **Removal of the need for micromanagement:** Where self-management occurs across the company, which in turn means that leaders have more energy and time to focus on what's important: working *on* the business rather than *in* the business.
- **Fully embedded culture:** The six embedding mechanisms all feed into living the values and delivering on the strategy of the company.
- **Interest from aligned investors:** The company's culture is recognized as an asset of the business and one of the reasons an investor invests in the business.
- **Differentiation:** The way the company communicates its vision, mission and values and how they are lived, stands out to potential employees and customers.
- **The gift of discretionary energy:** Where discretionary energy—the amount of time and effort that employees invest in the business when they're not officially "on the clock"—is given freely by employees.
- **Better overall performance:** As James L. Heskett wrote in his book *The Culture Cycle*, culture can account for 20-30 per cent of the differential in corporate performance when compared with 'culturally unremarkable' competitors.

HOW WE SENSE CULTURE

You will come across many companies in your lifetime. Thousands. Hundreds of thousands.

Whether as a CEO, founder, manager or employee, you will have noticed that not all companies are created alike. You'll buy products or services from them, partner with them, work for them, learn from them and sell to them. Some of them leave a bad taste in your mouth, like a rotten banana, anxiety or acid reflux. Other companies, on the contrary, leave you feeling delighted, warm and happy. You perform and finish your transactions with them and walk away *feeling better*.

Whether you work with or sell to other businesses or direct to consumers, your company's potential for success within a globalized, ever-more-competitive digital marketplace lies in its power to resonate deeply with the people buying and using your product. As consumers, we pay attention to which companies make us feel what emotions, and in today's world, we can broadcast that quite easily. From word-of-mouth recommendations to social media posts on Yelp or Glassdoor to reviews or complimentary tweets, we are happy to celebrate a company's strengths. The more a company resonates with us, the more we will tell others about it and give it our support. The opposite is also true, yet more so. People will actively avoid dealing with a company and tell a lot more people about it if they have a negative experience. Especially if that experience demonstrates that a company's values do not resonate with their own.

- **There's a reason why** you are intrigued when you hear that Charlie Kim, the cofounder and co-CEO of New York-headquartered Next Jump, mandates that his employees spend 50 percent of their time on culture development initiatives and 50 percent of their time on revenue-generating initiatives.
- **There's a reason why** Atlanta-based SalesLoft's parental leave policy includes a 12-month diaper subscription, has meal kit dinners for two delivered twice a week and pays for a bi-weekly home cleaning service twice per week for 12 weeks.
- **There's a reason why** Mark Organ, founder and Executive Chairman of Toronto-based Influitive, threatens to fire his employees if they don't take three weeks of vacation.
- **There's a reason why** people turn up at the office in pajamas at Chicago-based Jellyvision during Spirit Week in October, which is also the busiest time of their year.
- **There's a reason why** the fully-remote company Hotjar offers company perks that include 40 days of paid time off annually, 16 weeks paid parental leave, a $2,200/year holiday budget, a $4,400/year home office budget, a $2,600/year working space allowance, a $550/year personal development budget, a $2,200/year working together budget, a $2,600/year well-being allowance, a free Kindle Paperwhite and company retreats twice a year.

This encompassing reason is what many other ground-breaking and culture-driven companies—from seasoned giants to high-growth startups—have harnessed to break the mold, connect on a deeper level with their employees and customers and propel themselves to unparalleled heights of global success. This reason is the internal glue that binds such companies. It is a combination of a company's habits, behaviors, beliefs, principles, norms, mission, vision and values.

The reason is company culture.

Whether or not you've stopped to consciously think about it—and if not, take a minute and do so now—*you're more likely to do business with people you like.*

Like the 2018 Accenture Global Consumer Pulse, which surveyed 30,000 consumers from around the world, countless studies have proven this, as have your own past experiences and intuition. You tend to like the people with whom you resonate and who resonate with you. And you've most likely found yourself returning to companies and businesses whose employees embody their culture when you do business with them. They have the right attitude, good vibes, and an inherent commitment to delivering excellence and making you, their customer, happy. That's how we sense company culture.

We sense strong company culture in successful businesses when we work with their employees, use their services, or start using their products.

We also sense when it's weak. When companies don't invest in their culture, we pick up clues from unhappy employees, poor service, and the way the company treats us as customers. Consider a company like HubbleHQ, the London-based commercial real estate marketplace. HubbleHQ aims to delight its customers at every opportunity and empower them to make informed decisions, and one of the ways it does this is by making previously hidden industry data freely available. The company allows its customers to resonate with its culture through its interactions with them. These companies with strong cultures are the ones that we want to work for, work with, buy from, and help succeed.

Think about how unpleasant it was the last time you interacted with a company where it was patently obvious that the employees didn't care about what they were doing. How did you feel about them? What did you do next? Did it affect your future decisions to buy from that company?

WHY DON'T MORE CEOS TAKE ADVANTAGE OF THEIR CULTURE?

David Cummings founded Atlanta Ventures and the Atlanta Tech Village startup hub after selling Pardot to ExactTarget/Salesforce for $100 million in 2012. I asked Cummings how many of the Atlanta Tech Village portfolio companies he thought genuinely cared about nurturing and developing their company culture, and his answer was illuminating:

> "I espouse culture a lot and I would love more entrepreneurs to care and be more deliberate about it. But apart from a small percentage of founders who get it from the outset, the value of a deliberate and strong culture isn't driven home until a major challenge or serious setback occurs in the business. That's typically when I can point out how and why this challenge would have been avoided with a strong culture in place."

He added, "No matter how much I talk about it, many entrepreneurs really don't pay deep attention until it affects them. Once they feel the pain, though, they start listening very closely!" Cummings described an example of one of the companies he has been deeply involved in, SalesLoft. "It's an amazing business which is eight years old and has about 400 employees now. The first couple of years were a real challenge because culture wasn't a priority. We only focused down on the culture after experiencing the pain of unnecessary mishaps that happened in the business." Since they focused on the culture SalesLoft has won the Number 1 Top Places to Work in Atlanta (more about the SalesLoft culture later in this book). From a business point of view, the resulting growth, scale, and success speak for themselves. "It's a rocket ship business with an incredibly strong culture at its core."

CEOs who take advantage of their culture use it as a lens to evaluate every decision made inside the company. At a fundamental level, they question whether the decisions taken are adding to, or subtracting from the culture.

Aligning decision-making with the company's values, mission, and vision leads to committed and engaged people, higher growth, a faster route to sustainability and profitability, a stronger exit potential and a more memorable reputation than the competition. I hope that more CEOs will take advantage of their culture after reading this book.

WHO IS THIS BOOK FOR?

In *Culture Decks Decoded*, I wrote about three types of company CEOs and the different ways they approach company culture development. Since then, The examples, tools and techniques described in this book are applicable across all industries.I discussed this topic with Maarten Roerink, former CEO of Guidion. That conversation helped me realize that there are five archetypes when it comes to the different approaches CEOs take when developing their culture.

1. The **Culture Agnostic CEO** is not interested in wasting their time on company culture because they don't believe it's essential.
2. As the name suggests, the **Tick-Box CEO** treats company culture like a tick-the-box exercise, and once they have defined their values, mission and vision statements, they tick the box and forget about them.
3. The **Toe In The Water CEO** recognizes the importance of company culture and starts by defining the company's core values, mission and vision statements with the senior leadership team. A problem arises when the definition work done by the leadership team doesn't resonate with the rest of team. Something that happens regularly is the team disengages from the culture development effort because the CEO fails to take the next step of incorporating the values and culture into the functions, processes and systems of the business.
4. The **Culture Aware CEO** recognizes the importance of developing a strong culture and is prepared to invest time understanding, defining, embedding, reinforcing and managing their culture on an ongoing basis. This CEO is looking for new ideas to take their culture to the next level.
5. The **Transitioning To Remote or Hybrid CEO** is now realizing how much they took their previously undefined and unwritten office-based culture for granted. They now need to be deliberate and invest in their culture.

I wrote this book for companies led by the third, fourth and fifth CEO types. These CEOs understand, or in the case of the Transitioning To Remote CEO, are suddenly starting to understand the critical importance of developing a strong company culture. They want to build businesses where their people enjoy their work, fulfill their potential, and make a difference no matter where they work. They want to differentiate their company from the competition by communicating and sharing their business's uniqueness and greatness. They want to communicate their company's definition of what success looks like, how the company deals with failure, what the company looks for and how it attracts the best talent, why you should or shouldn't work there, how the company develops its people, and how they can grow, develop themselves, and self-actualize.

If you work for the first two types of CEO, please send them a copy of this book. It might just spark a light-bulb moment.

THE COMPANY CULTURE PRIORITY

The traditional operating model for business—characterized by linearity, hierarchy and a "slow and steady" growth rate to success—evolved during and for the Industrial Age. Change that occurred back then took place slowly and predictably; it was mostly toothless and perfectly suited to the complicated yet foreseeable challenges arising within that environment. The odd minor crisis would occasionally poke its head up due to changes in legislation or evolutionary shifts in the marketplace, and companies had time to deal with these issues. In general, businesses grew slowly, enjoying the luxury of time and allowing their culture to develop just as slowly and organically.

Today's world is stripped of such lenience.

Before December 2019, the digital revolution had launched an exponential rate of change that rendered many old business models and human processes useless. When was the last time you visited a physical store to have your photos printed or book a flight? When was your last trip to a video store? Every part of the economy was impacted by quantum leaps in technology and tectonic shifts in the competitive environment. Few industries were left untouched and new companies were formed as old companies struggled to adapt. A small percentage of these companies' leaders understood the importance of a strong, functional culture and went on to invest in and build, what I have termed, culture-driven companies. Companies such as Runway East, Jellyvision, busuu, Hotjar, Unbounce and Thread share one unwavering characteristic: they recognize culture as a critical asset of their companies. They treat it as such. The culture-driven CEOs of these companies openly state that their company's success is due in a large part to the strength of the culture they have built.

However, most business leaders failed to realize the extent to which culture played a role in the success of their businesses. They either decided that culture development was a waste of time, or that it wasn't urgent or important enough and put off developing their culture. Running an office-based business meant that these leaders could get away with not investing in or developing their culture. The CEO did not feel that he had to work on the company's culture because the team spent eight-plus hours together in the office. This proximity to the leaders and their colleagues gave people the chance to osmotically learn about the culture by listening for clues, watching, guessing, interpreting and assuming what the right and wrong things to do were. CEOs have gotten away with this approach... until now.

Nobody knows how long this new paradigm will last or what business as usual will look like when the COVID-19 pandemic is over. What we do know is the culture of every previous office-based business has changed irrevocably, overnight. The unwritten culture of the past could become a liability. To keep their people engaged, productive, motivated, committed and loyal, leaders who took their culture for granted will need to become intentional about developing a new culture that combines what worked in the past with the new reality of remote or hybrid work. The difference for these leaders is they will have to be deliberate about it. Apart from ensuring business survival and eventual success, the people challenge ahead is immense.

The culture-driven leaders interviewed for this book have an advantage and a head start on adapting to the new remote work or hybrid flexible work reality. These leaders have defined the cultural DNA of their business. They have documented their culture. They have integrated their values and behaviors into the processes and functions of the business. They and their teams understand and live the culture. They know the fundamental building blocks of their culture and will have a clear understanding of what elements of their culture can and can't be transferred across to the new paradigm. Even with a head start, the culture-driven leaders will have their work cut out for them. As you will read later in this book, developing a strong, functional high-performance remote or hybrid culture isn't easy.

COMPANY CULTURE: AN ASSET OR A LIABILITY?

A company culture cannot be described as good or bad or the best or worst, unless you are describing how an individual feels about that culture. If you were born into an organized crime family, you would most likely not have an issue solving problems using for-hire violence, because that's the way things have been done for generations. As an outsider, you probably find that behavior abhorrent and a totally unacceptable way to deal with someone whom you fall out with. How an individual feels is not an appropriate way to describe a company culture.

A company's culture can be strong or weak and functional or dysfunctional.

A strong culture is one where the values, mission and vision are:
- Understood, clearly defined and documented.
- Demonstrated and reinforced continuously.
- Lived by leadership and the entire team.
- Managed and evaluated regularly.
- The lens through which decisions are evaluated and made.

A weak culture is where the values, mission and vision have not been defined, or they have been defined but have not been integrated into the organization. The employees can't describe the culture consistently because they each interpret it in their own way and the behavior inside the company varies widely.

A company culture can also be functional, where the culture has a positive influence on the team and thereby performance of the company, or dysfunctional, where the culture has a negative influence on the performance. The aim of understanding, defining, embedding and managing your culture is to eliminate the dysfunctional elements of your culture while strengthening the functional elements.

Rather than asking "Is culture important?" or "Does culture make me money?" ask yourself, "How does a weak culture, or how does a dysfunctional culture destroy value?" If you fail to get your culture right, it doesn't matter how good your products are. It doesn't matter how slick your services may be. Yes, you may, through force of personality, be able to make the business work. But working in an environment like that is soul destroying and dealing with a company like that is painful, frustrating and disappointing. Over time you will lose your best people to companies with stronger, functional cultures and your customers will go the same way. That's because there's nothing to resonate with or connect to. There's nothing to fall in love with or get passionate about.

If done well, defining the company culture gives the team a common language. The culture becomes the guide to dealing with the uncontrollable and unexpected events that happen as a result of the volatile world in which we operate. A strong functional company culture is an asset that gives the team structural stability, group identity, and can provide meaning, predictability and agility. Culture provides the team a framework to make the right decisions and take the right actions in unforeseen situations, when you, the CEO, are not around. This is one reason why the remote leaders work so hard to develop a strong culture because in a remote working environment, the CEO is never around.

The opposite can be very painful. The CEO who fails to invest in his company culture is instead allowing a liability to develop and will:
- Work harder to lead the team.
- Struggle to hire and retain the best talent.
- Find it hard to differentiate the business in a highly competitive environment.
- Work harder to win and retain customers.
- Fail to build or extract the most value from the endeavor.

The company will be unlikely to ever fulfill the vast potential that convinced its employees and investors to come on board. That CEO is ignoring one of the most powerful business assets he has, instead allowing it to become a potentially serious liability.

CULTURE HAPPENS

Just as with an individual's character, culture happens outside of our awareness, below the surface. We recognize certain behaviors from that individual but can't see the forces at work below the surface. Just as our character drives our behavior as individuals, so too does culture drive the behavior of a company's employees. It's not simple to develop a strong company culture; like building a strong character, it takes awareness, practice and commitment.

Culture can be mistakenly underrated as gimmicky or brushed aside as an afterthought. Some leaders think it is enough to offer a few employee perks or tack up posters throughout the office that display so-called values. One common mistake is to perceive it as less significant than the finance, marketing or sales functions. From my research I have found that most CEOs consider culture to be something they'll get to when they have time. The problem with that approach is that culture happens whether you like it or not. What could be more essential and require more immediate action than something that permeates, is reflected in, and influences every aspect of the business? What could be more significant than the one sustainable competitive advantage which the CEO has total control over?

THE MISSING BUSINESS FUNCTION

What is company culture? In his seminal book *Organizational Culture and Leadership*, Edgar H. Schein defined culture as "a pattern of shared basic assumptions that a group has learned as it solved its problems of external adaptation and internal integration, that has worked well enough to be considered valued, and therefore, to be taught to new members as the correct way to perceive, think, and feel about those problems." In other words, culture forms when decisions that are made, prove to be successful, and the thinking that went into those decisions becomes embedded into "the way we do things around here." "The way we do things around here" is the accumulated learning that comes from the survival, development, growth and successful scaling up of a startup; it is essentially how your business operates at different stages of the lifecycle of the company.

It's essential to note that the way your business operates changes over time, which in turn means that your company culture changes over time. The way a team worked when eight people were trying to achieve a Minimal Viable Product was vastly different from the way they worked when there were 50 people in two offices starting to scale the business internationally. The way that team operates under pandemic-related restrictions is completely different again. Your company culture—your company's greatest asset—is constantly changing, and, as the leader, you need to understand how it is changing and what that means for your business. Contrary to what some leaders believe, culture is not a box to check; I believe that it needs to be constantly managed in the same way that sales, marketing and finance are.

I do not believe that every company with a well-defined culture is guaranteed to succeed.

Let me state categorically: I do not believe that every company with a well-defined culture is guaranteed to succeed. Far from it. I believe, backed up by research and business case studies, that companies with a well-defined culture have a greater chance of success than those without it, because they can nurture, evolve, and manage it, and realize the value of the asset it is. As we see, time and time again, companies that succeed in scaling a global multi-billion-dollar success invest heavily in their culture and the most successful ones do it early in the growth cycle.

Regardless of sector, niche, or the size of a business, it's company culture that is an ever-present element brimming with potential. It is a weapon that can be wielded to bring unprecedented success or self-sabotaging downfall. The anecdotes drawn from the interviews you'll read throughout this book demonstrate the ultimate pattern: the choice isn't whether to develop a culture or not, because you already have one; the choice lies in how explicit, tangible, purposeful and ultimately beneficial you want your company's culture to be.

According to a study by Deloitte, over 90 percent of business leaders agree that culture is critical to success. From my research, ninety percent of companies do not have a well-defined culture; hence culture development is the missing piece of the business puzzle. My mission is to help turn culture into a critical business function because culture is too influential to not take a seat at the top table. The travesty is that most business leaders don't know where to start or how to build a strong company culture, and therefore never do. This book aims to pry open the black box of culture and provide a guide for the founder, CEO, or business leader who wishes to be more intentional and deliberate about culture development.

There are more and more leaders who are reaping the benefits of a focus on company culture. The culture-driven companies they lead, companies that live their culture and make decisions based primarily on how those decisions align with the company's values, mission and vision are neither anomalies nor a passing trend. As we navigate through the next decade, the concept of a culture-driven business strategy—as *deliberately developmental organizations, sociocracy, lean, agile,* or however it is described and delivered—will become the norm.

Two primary components of a culture-centric perspective are already producing obvious market shifts and will continue to drive change:

- Individuals actively seek workplaces that prioritize their personal growth and development, and second, companies embracing culture-driven management have gained notable competitive advantage.
- The companies that excel in the future will be those that adopt a new insight and approach to human growth across their entire business, pursuing culture development as a collaborative, bottom-up and top-down strategy.

This book features lessons drawn from interviews conducted with over 50 business leaders including founders, CEOs and VPs of People Operations from the US, UK, and Europe. Each interaction proved to me how fundamental culture is as a business asset that leaders must invest in and how unusual it unfortunately still is that a startup or an established company recognizes culture as the missing piece of the business puzzle. The truly shocking statistic is that nine times out of 10, the startups I spoke with had nothing meaningful to articulate regarding their culture, which is why I had to speak to over 400 companies (and stopped counting) to secure 50 interviews. While nearly every leader I spoke with acknowledged the importance of culture, only 10 percent of these same companies bothered to address it. This small percentage, it turns out, automatically gifted themselves with an above-average chance of success and if they get through the challenging times ahead, it gives them an almost magical ability to scale rapidly and sustainably.

HOW TO USE THIS BOOK

This book will help to demystify company culture by supplying a framework for business leaders to build a strong, functional culture. As you read this book you will learn how culture-driven leaders use tools and techniques to incorporate their values deep within the functions and processes of their business, ensuring that their people are engaged in, committed to, and living the culture.

It's essential to remember that no two cultures are the same. Every company operates differently. You can't copy another culture, but you can borrow the tools and techniques that these companies use to develop their culture into a more visible, conscious and tangible asset. This book will guide you through the process to understand, define, embed, reinforce and manage your company culture. In each chapter you will find actionable examples that you can test and use in your organization immediately to start to surface your culture and unleash your people and your business's full potential.

Not all of the examples, tools and techniques in this book will be suitable for your culture or the culture you want to build. Choose those that resonate with you and that you think will work within your organization and test them out. If they work and enhance your culture, integrate them into your operating system; if they don't conduct a post-mortem, understand why they didn't, learn and move on. When it comes to culture development you need to use an experiment mindset, accept failures, nurture the ones with potential and double down on what works.

AND FINALLY...

Through the interviews and stories in this book I will demonstrate that your:

- Culture is either an asset or a liability.
- Culture is the core foundation to building and scaling a truly great business.
- Culture is magnetic and should attract the right people and repel the wrong people for your organization.
- Culture is the super glue for your team when the chips are down.
- Culture can only be affected by you and the people you

employ.
- Culture will differentiate you from the competition.
- Culture is hard to do right, but it will pay dividends.
- Culture takes leadership and needs to be both rigid and adaptable.
- Culture should be managed in the same way as any other business function, such as engineering, finance and sales.
- Culture is the one sustainable competitive advantage that you have complete control over.
- Culture doesn't guarantee success but a strong, functional culture will improve your chances of success.

Chapter 2

The Outcome of a Well-Defined Culture

"The only thing we have is one another. The only competitive advantage we have is the culture and values of the company. Anyone can open up a coffee store. We have no technology, we have no patent. All we have is the relationship around the values of the company and what we bring to the customer every day. And we all have to own it."
– Howard Schultz, former CEO, Starbucks

High-growth startups—what *is* it about them?

How do these underfunded, understaffed, under-resourced and high-risk ventures manage to compete for, win, and retain talent against the likes of Facebook, Google, Amazon, Microsoft and other such 700-pound gorillas?

Why did those early employees join Spotify in 2006? What drew the first 30 employees to a failing game development company called Tiny Speck, which eventually launched the hugely successful communication platform called Slack? What is the magic ingredient that makes an engineer or product manager decide to join a company without a viable product? Why would they accept a lower salary in a high-risk venture and work with a team that often has limited or no experience in a new and unproven market?

The leaders of high-growth companies with well-defined cultures have a better chance of attracting and retaining the best talent because they resonate on a deeper level with those people. Emotion is what pulses at the heart of culture. Emotion is visceral, immediate, evocative and timeless. The leaders of those companies are able to harness emotion by clearly articulating the values that overlap between the company and the candidate—in particular the mission, the vision and the greater purpose that all together make up their company culture.

If done properly, culture development requires daily commitment from the leadership team and awareness and engagement from everyone else.

Culture-driven companies have such a fierce competitive advantage because they've done the hard work to develop and nurture their culture. Culture must be designed and then managed; it can't be left to develop unchecked. Like any other business function, if done properly, culture development requires daily commitment from the leadership team and awareness and engagement from everyone else.

WHAT IS A WELL-DEFINED CULTURE?

Your competition can work to eliminate each of your business's competitive advantages by undercutting you on price, spending more money on marketing, hiring more people for more money, launching more features, and so on. Indeed, you have no control over what your competition may do. Still, there is one sustainable competitive advantage that you have complete control over, that they can't destroy: your company culture. Culture develops when decisions that are made prove to be successful, and the thinking that went into those decisions becomes embedded into "the way we do things around here." The way you compete, the way you acquire customers, the way you recruit, the way you onboard new employees, the way you hold meetings, the way you hire, fire, and promote, what you measure and control, what you reward and recognize—these all fuse together in a totally unique way to form your company's culture, the way that business learns to succeed.

A well-defined culture starts with the definition of a company's vision, mission and values statements. But most companies stop there. The team invests the time in defining their DNA and then don't do anything with it. A well-defined culture goes deeper, beyond the values, mission and vision statements into the inner layers of the onion. The behaviors associated with each value must be defined, and the stories associated with those values and behaviors need to be collected and shared. Symbols and rituals need to be defined and habitualized. Culture-driven companies go even further and define "the way we do things around here," which includes, but isn't limited to:

- Reward and recognition initiatives.
- Elements of the culture that leadership will pay attention to and measure.
- Learning and development initiatives.
- Values-based hiring, employee promotion guidelines, as well as what will get you fired.

A well-defined culture is one where the leadership team views decision-making through the lens of the values and behaviors, which are also deliberately integrated into the business's functions and processes.

CULTURE REQUIRES CONSISTENCY

Culture-driven CEOs realize that culture is never done. They define their culture, embed it, and refine it, viewing culture development as an iterative process. Alicia Navarro, cofounder and President of Skimlinks, spent a significant amount of time—as much as 50 percent at times—focused on culture development—a sentiment echoed by every CEO and founder featured in this book. These leaders realize that spending time thinking about and developing their culture has a real return on investment. One of the returns on the investment is to free up time—allowing them some breathing room and the ability to focus on what's important, rather than what's urgent. In fact, culture-driven leaders come to understand that culture development isn't just *a priority*—it should be *the number one priority*. Nicolas Dessaigne, cofounder of Algolia the Search-As-A-Service platform, described this perfectly when we spoke about how to balance culture development and company growth. "Culture is a living organism and I don't think you can ever fully figure everything out. If you do it's only temporary because what you have figured out will only stay relevant for a relatively short period of time, especially if you are scaling. That's been our experience, anyway." Explaining his thinking on prioritizing culture he said, "If you don't put culture first, by default it's going to be second. As soon as you don't keep it top of mind, you may not see what is really happening in the business." As I explain later in the book, Dessaigne has made the mistake of not prioritizing culture and has, as a result, had to work hard to make up for the culture debt Algolia incurred during that time.

This realization often happens once the company has achieved traction and has made the typical mistakes associated with not defining their culture early on. For companies in the very early stages there are, of course, the realities associated with keeping the business alive; however, I believe that the companies that start to invest in their culture from day one, or at an early stage, place themselves in a better position to succeed than those that don't. Zappos founder and CEO Tony Hsieh hit the nail on the head when he said, "Our whole belief is that if you get the culture right, most of the other stuff—like delivering great customer service or building a long-term enduring brand—will just happen naturally on its own."

From attracting "unaffordable" talent, to making better decisions faster, to attracting the right investors, or saving millions of dollars in recruitment fees, in this chapter I explore examples of the competitive advantages that accrue to a company with a well-defined culture. The companies in this chapter work hard to make sure that their culture is well defined and that their values are clear and understood. Adaptive Insights achieved a $1.5 billion exit by developing a team that is highly aligned with the purpose and the vision of the company. Unbounce demonstrates its culture of transparency by over-sharing the company financials. Soundstripe developed a culture deck, almost on day one, to define and explain its culture's meaning. HubbleHQ was able to improve the pace of its decision-making by trusting its employees more. Evonomix's CEO uses the company values to give people more responsibility and hence he micromanages less. Skimlinks built a hacker-like culture and used a toaster in its open plan office to give a homey and safe feeling. Time:matters discovered the value of working with like-minded investors who understand culture's value.

1. Adaptive Insights

Tom Bogan is an excellent example of a leader who understands how to build and harness the power of a strong culture and conjure up that magic. Bogan, the CEO of San Francisco–based Adaptive Insights, has spent two decades in C-suite roles at high-growth tech companies, including being President and COO of Rational Software, which was acquired for $2.1 billion in 2003. He was also Board of Directors Chairman at Citrix Systems for over 10 years. He was a Partner at Greylock and over the last decade has filled numerous board level roles at companies like Apptio, PTC, Rally Software, and Black Duck Software. Bogan joined Adaptive Insights, a leading cloud-based software company that is modernizing business planning, as CEO in 2015. Under his leadership the business scaled from $40 million to over $100 million in revenue in two years, and he was literally days away from taking the company public in 2018 when Workday swooped in and acquired the business for $1.5 billion. Bogan believes that cultural alignment is the one thing that is present in all successful high-growth companies, and at Adaptive Insights Bogan was able to take the positives from the culture the founders had built and reinforce values, such as transparency and accountability, that he felt were necessary to scale the business to the next level.

When I asked him about the impact of a strong company culture, Bogan explained, "Something powerful happens in successful teams; there is this incredible sense of alignment and shared context. Having a team that is highly aligned with the purpose and the vision of the company is what allows it to achieve greatness. The people on the team know what's important, what the values are, and what matters within the company—whether that is how we treat employees or customers, or how we show respect for each other, or how we make decisions."

2. Evonomix

Evonomix, a marketing technology company headquartered in Constanța, Romania, is the brainchild of founder and co-CEO Mihai Bocai, whose evolving approach to developing and leading the company parallels the company's challenges and success. In the early days, Bocai admitted that he, like many first-time entrepreneurs, used to impose his ideas with an "It's my company and I know better" approach. He eventually realized that this micromanaging mentality was holding the company back. "That worked for a while," he said, "and the business grew initially, but eventually started to plateau. I came to the realization that I had to think seriously about developing the culture because the business wouldn't scale if I didn't empower my people."

As part of a companywide culture development program, Bocai and the team created a set of six values for the company: *growth and learning, transdisciplinarity, novel and adaptive thinking, integrity, innovate fast,* and *drive evolution through change.* Bocai said that the values really allowed him to move to the next level as a CEO. The six values they developed allowed Bocai to let go and give people more responsibility. He found that employees automatically stepped up to the plate. "The values have become the guiding principles of the business; they've allowed me to let go and they've empowered our people to use them as a framework to make decisions. The team are taking a lot more responsibility, I get a lot more feedback and great ideas, and the rate of growth, which slowed, has picked up again." In turn, this enabled Bocai to focus more on the strategy and not get caught up with urgent day-to-day situations that previously took up a lot of his time. The company has reaped tremendous benefits from the shift to a culture-driven environment. "We have a higher trust factor across the company, and our people are happier. On the recruitment side, we hire people who are better suited for the business and our staff turnover is lower than it's ever been. Another signal that the culture development program is working is the excellent feedback we get from customers."

3. HubbleHQ

Tushar Agarwal and Tom Watson are the cofounders of HubbleHQ, a London-based online marketplace that finds homes for companies by matching those looking to rent office space with those who have it. They realized the impact of HubbleHQ's culture extremely early. When I first sat down with them, their business had just grown from 8 to 18 employees within the span of three months. Doubling headcount (and then some) in such a short time frame is always challenging; it can be particularly dangerous for such a young startup.

"We started to feel the pain of rapidly scaling up the team as we kicked into hiring mode," they acknowledged. "We could see that we needed to clarify the culture for the new team members in order to make sure that everyone was on the same page, and to bond the team together. There were times when new members were confused as to how to make the right decision or what tone to use when addressing customers—how much to give versus holding their position. Going through the culture definition process illuminated to the team what our expectations were, how we were positioning our product, and how we needed to be talking to the customers."

The greatest impact of deeply embedding HubbleHQ's culture into the business, they told me, appeared in the dramatically improved pace of decision-making. By trusting and empowering their team to make decisions, Agarwal and Watson found that they were collectively able to make better decisions faster across every function or department of the business. "We are going so far as to build our three values—*empowerment*, *empathy*, and *experience*—into our product," they explained to me. Knowing these values and what they stand for, any employee can immediately answer the question "Does developing this feature match with one or more of our values?" and then make a decision based on how the feature is in line with the three values.

HubbleHQ's value of *empowerment* helped them make the decision to go against industry norms by offering their customers live pricing data. "We have won a lot of goodwill by empowering customers who tell us that they are glad we exist because we show live pricing in a sector where pricing is normally hidden. Empowerment means giving the customers as much relevant data as possible to make the right decision. Living our culture and building it into our product is one of the reasons they keep coming back to us."

Tom Bogan, Mihai Bocai, Tom Watson and Tushar Agarwal all recognize the value of culture to align their teams around what's essential, what matters within the company, and specifically around decision-making. The long-term success of any company is largely dependent on the ability of the broader team to make decisions. Because the leadership team can't and shouldn't be involved in every decision, you need to be confident that your team will make more of the right decisions and learn from making the wrong ones.

4. Skimlinks

The content monetization platform Skimlinks took small but vital steps when building its company culture to make employees comfortable at the office, attracting top-tier talent it wouldn't have otherwise been able to recruit. The company is the industry leader in affiliate marketing solutions, used by millions of websites and tens of thousands of publishers. By automatically affiliating links in content, the platform helps publishers monetize their editorial content; by syndicating the resulting behavioral data for advertisement use, it enables marketers to find clients far more efficiently. My discussion with Skimlinks cofounder and President Alicia Navarro left me with a reinforced appreciation of company culture and how, if you design the right environment for your people, you will be able to attract and retain outstanding employees.

Each of the CEOs and founders I spoke with for this book emphasized to me that developing a strong company culture requires an investment in time but doesn't necessarily require excess cash, especially in the early days of the business. It is a matter of purpose, a labor of love, and a belief in a long-term and extremely valuable investment. And this investment circles back to them with generous rewards. Navarro's emphasis on building a strong culture from the outset resonates in my mind. She said, "I instinctively understood the importance of building a strong culture. The Skimlinks culture has, from the very beginning been inviting, inclusive, innovative, hacker-like, compassionate and human." An example of Navarro's thinking and efforts to enhance the culture happened when they moved into new offices and deliberately designed aspects of the office to make it feel more like home. "We have the kitchen in the center of our open plan office, and we deliberately placed the toaster in the middle of the kitchen so the smell of toast—a smell of home and safety and happiness—infuses the office. This may seem like a small detail, but they all add up to form our #skimlove DNA."

This type of thinking and attention to detail about company culture demonstrates to potential employees how committed the company is to build a strong culture, and it paid off handsomely. "Like most startups, during the early stages of the business we could not afford to pay market-related salaries, but we did need the right talent to grow. Our culture enabled us to attract and hire outstanding candidates who we would not have expected to be able to afford. People, many of whom are still with the business today, wanted to work for us that much that they took a cut in their salaries." The opportunity for these executives to "own" a small piece of the company through stock options certainly helped. Skimlinks would not have grown to take the leadership position it did, if it weren't for these key early employees. By the same token, these employees would not have joined the business at such an early high-risk stage, if Navarro had not been able to demonstrate that the culture she was building at Skimlinks was right for them.

In this example Navarro uses a toaster to give her people a sense of home, safety and happiness. If you are building a remote or hybrid culture, try flipping this idea around and think about the initiatives you can implement to reconnect the people who are now working from home to the people, emotions, feelings and experiences they had while at the office.

5. time:matters

A clearly defined company culture can also serve as a magnet to attract the right investors and repel the wrong ones. Money is a commodity after all, and the right investors—those who are aligned with or understand your values, mission and vision—will comprehend why you might make a decision that will have a negative impact on cash flow in the short-term, but is the right decision for the business in the long-term. In 2001, Franz-Joseph Miller founded time:matters, a spin-off of Lufthansa Cargo AG. Miller launched time:matters as a technology and services platform offering same-day deliveries and global high speed logistics for the delivery of time-critical spare parts, large machines, highly urgent documents, unique prototypes or sensitive specimens.

The secret to attracting the right investors, Miller confided, turned out to be the culture. "We took investment from a private equity (PE) firm, and in preparation of our management presentation I decided to add a slide detailing our culture. The investment bank executives we were working with were unimpressed, saying that the PE firms wouldn't be interested in such soft topics. I told them that if that was the case, then we didn't want to talk to, or take investment from those firms. It turns out that a few of the investors were impressed with our story and our conviction and commitment to our culture. They realized that one of the main reasons for our success and the reason we were able to weather the business challenges we had, was *because* of our culture." There are times when a culture-driven CEO will make a decision that doesn't necessarily make sense when viewed through the lens of short-term commercial gain. Miller's advice is that companies should, where possible, work with likeminded investors who understand the importance of building a strong culture and then living up to the values, mission and vision. His PE backers understood the value of making decisions based on how they aligned with the company values and were subsequently rewarded for their commitment to the time:matters culture as Lufthansa Cargo acquired the company for a significant multiple on their original investment.

A minority of investors truly get culture. The investors with a long enough track record will have experienced the pain when a culture goes bad and will be able to recognize some of the patterns of a strong company culture. But very few venture capitalists (VCs) understand how to develop and manage a strong company culture. Even fewer understand how to build a remote work company culture. This will change over time as investors realize that an authentic culture that is lived by the team is critical to the success of the company. In the meantime, it's a real bonus if your investors have some understanding of the critical importance of a strong company culture. If you are living the values, you and your team will be making decisions based on how the expected outcome of those decisions matches the values of the business. They may not always appear to be the right decisions to someone who doesn't understand your culture.

Alicia Navarro and Franz-Joseph Miller demonstrate the impact a culture can have on being able to attract the right people, whether employees or investors. We know that remuneration is not the most influential aspect for most people when deciding to join a company. Having a well-defined culture allows you to connect on a different level with a candidate, moving the conversation away from money and allowing them to make a more informed decision. Taking investment from a VC or PE firm is a lot like getting married, it's just much harder to get a divorce. Getting the right investor on board, who understands from the beginning that developing a strong culture is vital, and that decision-making will be based on how that decision fits with the values of the company is essential. Just like a marriage you want to ensure that there is strong alignment and understanding about what's important.

6. Unbounce

Rick Perreault is the CEO and one of six cofounders of Unbounce, a Canadian software company that has built a landing page and conversion marketing platform allowing marketers to quickly create, launch and test high-converting landing pages and website overlays without the need for developers. Unbounce has enjoyed tremendous success since its launch in 2009, and Perreault believes that the culture has had a significant part to play in that success. He explained that writing down the values and garnering the team's collective approval and agreement was an instrumental move that allowed everybody to embody the culture actively and, crucially, ensured that no one was working against it.

One of their core values is transparency, which Perreault said had a major impact on developing a well-defined culture. By truly living the transparency value they were able to differentiate the company, making it more attractive to candidates, which has saved the company millions of dollars over the years. They demonstrate their transparency not only by sharing the company financials with new employees when they join, or with the whole company in their monthly Town Hall meetings, but they also share them with the broader community. "Outside of what we share with the Unbounce team, we write a blog post once a year and share the business's financials with the wider community." Sharing the financials on the company blog is a great example of how living the transparency value can have a positive impact on the business. As Perreault explained, "Just like most major tech cities, hiring is very competitive in Vancouver, and we have had situations where candidates have chosen Unbounce over other companies because we deliver on our transparency value in this way."

In the 12 months before we spoke, the company had grown by more than 100 employees and opened their third international office. The company had experienced less than one percent turnover in staff, and 99 percent of new hires had been made without the assistance of a recruiter. Perreault said that excluding the savings that accrued from not having to rehire, retrain, and onboard new employees, the Unbounce culture had helped attract and hire right candidates that fit their values *and* saved the company around $1.5 million in recruitment fees alone.

Unbounce doesn't have to share its financials with the public, but it does. Transparency helps to foster trust, which is one of the reasons they can convince candidates who are considering roles at other companies to join Unbounce.

Your business can become a magnet that attracts the right type of person by demonstrating that you and your team truly live the values. Trust is also a critical component for successful remote working. A company that operates without trust requires micromanagement. Not only is micromanagement difficult to do when your people are working from home, it's incredibly destructive toward their morale and motivation. You don't know what personal issues your people are dealing with while working from home. Being able to empathize, trust your people to deal with those issues, as and when they need to, and then deliver the output required, is vital. If your company has built a culture of trust through transparency, like Unbounce, then your business is well positioned to adapt and take advantage of a remote or hybrid work environment.

7. Soundstripe

Nashville-based Soundstripe's mission is to "Keep Creatives Creating," and the team achieves this by providing access to a collection of royalty-free music for an "unbeatable" price to video content creators. The company was recently voted as one of the top 10 best startup cultures to work for in Nashville. I asked founder and co-CEO Travis Terrell what he thought the impact of a strong company culture was on his company and his response was unequivocal. "It impacts everything! Defining and nurturing the culture early on has had a profound impact at Soundstripe." Not only did Terrell decide to define the culture in the early stages of the company, he also started to pull together a culture deck. Even though his team thought he was crazy Terrell said, "The deck was solidified, finished, and released about six months after launching the company, even though we only had a very small team at that point of about five people." The Soundstripe culture deck does an excellent job of explaining the meaning of its 10 values and how the company uses the values as a filter for every decision, covering such topics as how the company deals with confrontation, how the company focuses on quality not quantity, when to quit a project, and what type of person the company hires or lets go. Having the culture deck in place early on has allowed Soundstripe to grow the team very effectively.

The Soundstripe culture deck is available online[1] for everyone to view and the hiring team to use its contents as a guide to evaluate and filter candidates during the interview process. All candidates being considered for a role at Soundstripe must be able to articulate why they resonate with the company's mission to "keep creatives creating" and are a fit with the 10 core values described in detail in the online document.

As Terrell explained, "We are 56 people strong and zero people have quit at this point, which is amazing. That is an indicator to us that we have built this culture to be positive for our employees and our customers." He added, "To me it's so funny that leaders only think of their company culture later in the journey. I'm so glad that we were able to solidify ours early on because it gets harder to retain the people and the culture once you move into growth mode and start to implement new processes. Our culture has also allowed us to grow quickly without having the painful departmental fallouts that often happen."

Documenting your culture is a vital part of developing an effective culture. It is critical, as the leader of a company transitioning to a remote or hybrid work culture, for you to document your vision, mission, values and other unwritten or implied elements of the way you work. Your people are not going to be able to learn osmotically about your culture in the same way they did when the business was office-based. Not documenting your culture leaves your culture open to interpretation, misunderstanding and miscommunication. You can download a free PDF version of my first book *Culture Decks Decoded*.

In the last two examples Rick Perreault and Travis Terrell demonstrate the impact a strong culture can have on building and retaining your team. Whether it's growing rapidly, eliminating or reducing staff turn-over, saving millions of dollars on recruitment fees or hiring people who are a better fit with the values of the company, a well-defined culture gives your company a distinct advantage.

IN CONCLUSION...

On the surface, perhaps many company cultures look and sound the same—*trust, transparency, respect, accountability, authenticity,* and so forth—but they aren't. Each has its own DNA and later in this book I explain how culture-driven leaders define that DNA in the form of expected behaviors. Each is as distinctive as a fingerprint, and the CEOs interviewed in this chapter demonstrate a clear understanding of how to leverage their culture, their unique competitive advantage to:

- Scale the business to a successful exit.
- Recruit A+ talent (with limited financial resources).
- Give people more responsibility.
- Empower their employees and their customers.
- Demonstrate and harvest transparency.
- Save millions of dollars on recruitment fees.
- Increase the speed of decision-making.
- Attract like-minded investors.

By demonstrating that their businesses have a deep-seated commitment to invest in and live their culture, these culture-driven leaders are harnessing their culture as a unique selling point and significant differentiator, and the impact is clear.

Chapter 3

The Sooner You Start The Better

"In our early years, we didn't talk about culture much. But the real return on culture happened when we started getting more deliberate about it. By writing it down. By debating it. By taking it apart, polishing the pieces, and putting it back together. Iterating. Again. And again."
– Dharmesh Shah, Cofounder, Hubspot

When should you start to work on defining your company culture? The short answer is: ASAP. It comes down to this simple fact: the longer you wait to define your culture, the more cultural debt you build up, and the harder it gets.

Whether it's a mindful process or not, the evolution of your culture is unavoidable. One key difference between company cultures lies in their origin stories: an undefined or neglected culture develops unconsciously by default, not by design. Bad habits, behaviors and practices that build up to form the cultural debt creep in with the good as the company progresses and the team grows. Reversing or undoing these unwanted habits, behaviors and practices is extremely difficult once they become ingrained into the "way we do things around here," especially if they appear—at least on the surface or for the short term—to be working. These cracks inevitably become fault lines once the company starts to scale. Similarly, they become serious fault lines when a company is forced to adopt remote work practices.

The sooner you define your culture the sooner you can start to nurture and develop it into the asset it has the potential to be. The sooner you define your culture the sooner you can be explicit about the behaviors you expect from your team. The sooner you define your culture the sooner you embed it into the functions, processes and policies of the business, the sooner your team can start to live them and hold one another accountable to living them.

This chapter discusses what vision statements, mission statements and values are and their importance in building company culture. I then dive more deeply into the different ways that values are built and strengthened in companies.

In this chapter I look at how the Unbounce and Thread founders build a positive and strong culture from the outset. Busuu realized that culture isn't a tick-box exercise and that it needed to be more explicit about its values. The founders of Influitive developed core values before incorporating the company. Skimlinks created a unique company language revolving around its values. Periscope Data prioritized three of its eight values, and Emarsys created a culture committee consisting of people with high EQ to help evolve its culture.

WHERE TO BEGIN WHEN DEVELOPING YOUR CULTURE

1. Start with Your Cofounder(s)

In a company's early days, it pays to make sure that you and your cofounder(s) have similar motivations and reasons for starting the business. Nic Brisbourne, Managing Partner at Forward Partners, a venture fund–meets–startup studio says it's "depressingly common" for founding teams, just like married couples, to not go the distance. Lawyering up to try to extract the "wrong" cofounder is an expensive and time-consuming exercise that can, and often does, lead to the destruction of the business.

Once you have ascertained that you and your cofounder(s) are on the same page and heading in the same direction, you should work together to agree upon the values, mission and vision statements for the business. Having an in-depth conversation about the culture you want to build this early and putting pen to paper helps to set the right foundations in place for the business as it grows.

2. As You Prepare to Scale the Business

It is preferable that you define your culture before you start to scale the business aggressively. High-growth companies will often raise a large amount of venture capital funding to help scale the business once the product market fit, sizable addressable market, and sustainable commercial traction have been proven. The founders, who are used to running the business on a shoestring budget, can be unprepared for the myriad of challenges that arise at this stage of growth. One of the main challenges is the pressure to grow the team, which can lead to desperation to hire people quickly. It's pretty much impossible to consistently hire people with the right functional skills and experience, who are also a good fit with the values of the company, if the culture has not been defined at this stage. As the team doubles or triples in size, the founders find that they are no longer able to connect with each person in the same way they once did. Over time the original unwritten culture that developed as a result of being in close proximity to the founders becomes diluted into an accidental collection of good and bad behaviors. Because the team is bigger and the founders are stretched, they are no longer able to demonstrate to everyone in the team how they should behave, and the bad behaviors become embedded into the culture.

3. Pandemic-Enforced Remote Working Scenario

If you had not defined your culture before the current pandemic, it is critical that you start to do so now. You are forming a new culture, whether you like it or not. The way your team operates has changed radically and your team is learning new ways of working, and as a result of that, you are going to have to deal with many new challenges like loneliness, anxiety, burnout, and disengaged and unmotivated employees to name but a few. New assumptions, norms, habits and behaviors—both good and bad—are being developed. It is impossible in a remote environment and harder in a hybrid work environment for your team to learn osmotically about what is acceptable and unacceptable behavior. It is also much harder to recognize police and stamp out bad behavior in the way you might have done in an office environment . Defining and documenting your culture will start to give your team the structure and guidelines they need to work effectively, and help new joiners get up to speed.

Some of the leaders mentioned in this chapter began to discuss and define their culture on day one, others started in the first month of founding their business, and others became deliberate about their culture three years into their business. The longer you take the harder it can be, but no matter how long you have been in business, it's vital that you start to do it now.

VISION STATEMENTS, MISSION STATEMENTS AND VALUES

In its simplest form culture can be stripped down to the combination of vision statements, mission statements and the values of the company. Some companies make use of a mission or a vision statement combined with their values. I believe that a company should have both, because the values, mission and vision are interconnected. The values (the how) drive the behavior of the team as they deliver on the day-to-day requirements of fulfilling the mission (the what). By fulfilling the mission, the team gets closer to achieving the vision (the why).

The Vision Statement

A company's vision articulates **why** the company exists and the business's medium- to long-term goals and aspirations. Looking five to ten years into the future, if everything goes right, this is how the company will change the world. To be powerful and inspiring it should be compelling, meaningful, and boldly ambitious, capturing the Why, and what the company could make happen if anything were possible. An effective vision statement is ideally one or at most two sentences long. The Vision Statement should be the responsibility of the leader or leadership team.

1. Unbounce

Rick Perreault and the other cofounders of Unbounce started talking about their culture on day one. They all had experiences at companies that weren't the best places to work, where leaders didn't invest in the culture, and where employees were treated like commodities. "We all knew what it felt like to work in a weak company culture, so we set out to build a positive and strong one from the outset. Initially our culture evolved and developed organically; we didn't define or write down what our culture was but we knew that we shared the same vision. We started to really focus on defining our culture and work environment when we reached about 30 or 40 people. We knew we were going to continue to grow rapidly, and in order to do that effectively and efficiently we needed to have our culture, and what it meant, clearly defined." As part of that process Unbounce made sure to start by spelling out the vision statement: *Unbounce exists to empower every business to create better marketing experiences.*

The Mission Statement

A company's mission statement describes the organization's visible, tangible work in the world—**what** the company does, who it does it for, and how this helps that client. It explains the tangible activities and overall approach or attitude the company takes as it translates the big picture vision into everyday action. The mission statement can be more collaborative and include members of the broader team.

2. Algolia

Nicolas Dessaigne is the cofounder and former CEO of Algolia, the hosted web search software company that provides product teams with the resources and tools they need to create fast, relevant searches. When we spoke, Dessaigne said that historically the company didn't have much in the way of an official mission statement. They tried to introduce one, but Dessaigne didn't think it was that crucial and was never happy with anything they came up with. "I thought, no one works somewhere because of the mission statement." He came to see, however, that having a clear mission about what the company does is vital to the team. "How wrong I was. I realized that everything people do is attached in some way to the mission—not only in the sense of the outside world, but internally, too, within the company. When you fully understand what the company is doing, you are more confident of what needs to be done and are therefore prepared to take more risks to get things done." Clearly articulating your mission demands you do some fundamental work up front. From this he created Algolia's mission statement: *Our mission is to enable every developer and product team to build consumer-grade search.*

Dessaigne's experience is not an anomaly; all too often leaders instinctively know where they're going and mistakenly conclude that everyone else around them can read their minds and know the same things. As he explained, "There's a moment when you openly discuss what you think everyone knows and you see people's eyes widen. You realize that it's on you; you hadn't communicated the message clearly or repeated it enough times to make it stick."

If the company values are not well crafted, then the values of the person and the way they interpret the company values drive their individual behaviors.

The Values

Belonging is a fundamental requirement of the human condition. We need to belong to create a sense of reality and to find meaning in what we do. The personal values of a new member of the team must align with the company's values for them to become a fully integrated member of the team and thereby fulfill their need to belong. Until they become part of the team and feel like they belong, they are essentially outsiders and are not able to give 100 percent of themselves to the company. This is critical for onboarding new employees, which I will cover later in the book.

Your employees have one of two choices every time they enter the office and sit down at their desks.

1. If their values are aligned with the company's values, they can be themselves, be part of the team, and apply 100 percent of themselves to your company's challenges, with creativity, commitment and enthusiasm.

2. If their values do not align with the company's values, they must somehow leave that part of them that is misaligned outside the office. When they do enter the office, they come in with a façade that attempts to fit in with the team, and they spend time trying to be someone they aren't. The problem with a façade is that it's not natural and it takes effort and energy to keep the mask from slipping. When a person's values are not aligned with the company's values it is not possible for them to deliver their best, ultra-high performance. They must continually regulate their actions and behaviors to make sure that they stay within the bounds of the company's value structure. Due to the misalignment, that employee

is leaving 10, 25 or 30 percent of their capacity and inventiveness to be fully engaged in your business, at the door.

Developing company values that resonate with you and the team is the critical first step to building a strong and functional company culture. Values describe what's important to the business with respect to **how** it operates, the people it hires and the customers it serves. If well crafted, the values guide and drive the behaviors of the individuals that make up the team. In this way the values get everyone rowing at the same speed and in the same direction. Your list of values can include both current and aspirational values. It is essential to remember that the list of values should be inclusive; everyone in the company should be able to live, or aspire to live, the values—if not all the time, then most of the time.

In this section, I explore the different ways that leaders approach defining their values, how they define those values, how they make them memorable, the mistakes they've made, and how to prioritize core values from an extended list.

3. Thread

Some CEOs believe that values aren't crucial in the early stages of the business and think they can delay defining their culture. Kieran O'Neill, cofounder and CEO of Thread and a serial entrepreneur since the ripe old age of 15, disagrees. He sold his first company, HolyLemon.com, a video-sharing company akin to YouTube, when he was 19 years old, and went on to cofound and sell Playfire, a video game social network that had grown to over 1 million users. Thread is an online personal styling service, and its uniqueness is embodied in its fusion of algorithms and AI with real-life stylists. The company's team is tied together by a vibrant work culture and a shared purpose to enable customers to "dress well without trying."

O'Neill told me that culture development was an intentional process within Thread from the very beginning. O'Neill and his cofounder Ben Philips had a clear idea of what they wanted to build culture-wise. Around the second week of business, they wrote down, at a high-level, what they wanted the culture to be like. O'Neill explained, "I then initiated a conversation with the team where we discussed company culture and defining our values as a set of guiding principles for the company. We all came together with different ideas and wrote them up on the white board, coming up with about 30 adjectives. The process from there was to discuss and debate them. I think we whittled it down to 10 or 12 ideas in that first session. We came back together in a second session and narrowed the list again to our seven values." The timing of defining a company's culture is also significant to O'Neill. "From my experience, the easiest time to introduce values is obviously at the start of the business when you have a clean sheet of paper. Trying to change a culture midway through building the business is much harder than actually doing the work at the beginning."

The team narrowed their list down to a set of seven values by which they would run the business.

1. *Be user-experience obsessed:* We believe the only way to scale to hundreds of millions of people is if your product is 10x better than what existed previously.
2. *Be uncomfortably fast:* As a team we are prepared to tolerate discomfort by moving aggressively to achieve more in a given timeframe.
3. *Practice extreme clarity:* We empower people with information to enable them to make the right decision without management present. We prioritize ruthlessly.
4. *Practice extreme candor:* It requires true courage to hold each other accountable. Constructive conflict is often the sign of a healthy, mature team.
5. *Commit relentless self-iteration:* We place great emphasis on improving ourselves at both the individual and company level.
6. *Enjoy the journey together:* We only invite people to join the Thread team if we think they'll be travelers who'll enrich our journey. This manifests in kindness, support and empathy.
7. *Act like an owner:* The only way to sustain a strong culture is if everyone in it is fighting for it. Everyone must feel ownership. We are not looking for passengers.

Because of his two previous ventures, O'Neill understands how advantageous defining your company culture early in the business's life cycle can be. As you will read later in the book, he has used this foundation to build a company recognized for its strong and functional culture.

4. busuu

Bernhard Niesner is the cofounder and CEO of busuu, a London-based digital learning platform committed to developing innovative ways in which people can use technology to learn languages. I wanted to understand the process that he went through to define the values, mission and vision for busuu, and Niesner explained that in the early days the values were more implicit than explicit. The company was founded in Spain and relocated to the UK, which was when he and the team started to focus more on the culture. "Once we moved the company over to London and started to grow the team, we realized that we had to differentiate ourselves in the more competitive UK market, and the first step was to be more explicit about our values."

The leadership team sat down and created the list of values that represented the types of people they wanted to work with and the type of company they wanted to build. "This turned out to be more of a theoretical tick-box exercise because we unfortunately didn't apply the values to the day-to-day running of the company or embed them into our processes." This proved to be a big mistake for Niesner when the company went through an incredibly challenging period. "The business went through a tough patch and as soon as things got tough for the business, people started to leave. This was the first indication that we had hired the wrong people and I realized that most of the people we had hired did not match the values of the company." After coming through the challenging period, where a lot of the team left the company, Niesner decided to dust off the values and really integrate them into the business. Since then he has rebuilt the busuu team with people who really match the company's values.

"The list initially consisted of four values: *Trust, Effectiveness, Ambition* and *Curiosity*, which very much matched to who I am and the team I wanted to build. Being Austrian I believe in effectiveness and efficiency; as an entrepreneur I have always had great ambition;

trust is a key principle for me in business and in my personal life; and I am a curious person by nature. I also decided to add *Happiness* to the values list after the difficult period for the business, as I realized that I didn't want to spend time with negative people. I wanted to build an environment that encourages happiness."

Acronyms often help with learning and recollection, and the T.E.A.C.H. acronym fits well with a company that is innovating in the language learning space. Their core values are:

1. *Trust:* Be honest and respectful. Accept freedom and responsibility. Deliver on your promises.

2. *Effectiveness:* Solve the right problem. Move fast and get shit done. Empower our customers.

3. *Ambition:* Think big. Go the extra mile. Leave a legacy.

4. *Curiosity:* Question the status quo. Test, measure, learn and share. Strive to become a better version of yourself.

5. *Happiness:* Bring your passion. Help others succeed. Celebrate the team.

The mistake Niesner made by doing a "tick-box exercise" happens to too many founders because the work has only just begun once you've written the values, the mission and the vision statements. You don't stop managing the finance function once the budget has been created; in the same way defining the values, vision and mission is the first step on the journey of creating a strong and functional company culture.

5. Influitive

As I mentioned in Chapter 1, Mark Organ, founder and Executive Chairman of B2B marketing advocacy platform Influitive, launched his second company armed with his own history of experiences, accomplishments and lessons learned. At Eloqua, the first company he founded, he realized that his focus on the customer before the employee was a mistake, as was his failure to invest in the culture early on. Organ waited five years into the development of the business before becoming deliberate about the culture. Influitive is his second chance "to right some of the wrongs" he committed at Eloqua.

Even before incorporation, he sat down with a cofounder and two employees to discuss the company's culture. They started with core values "that were important to us, particularly regarding the people we wanted to attract to our young company." They recognized these values would become the foundation on which they would construct the mission and vision. Although not set in stone, the values, unlike the culture, should not necessarily change very often. However, it is critical to ensure that your values are relevant and in sync with your culture. Organ and the team initially created a list of nine values for the company, which was shortened to four after a later review. Organ explained, "We brought in a consultant to take us through a values review exercise and have slimmed down from nine values to four core values." Apart from being tough to remember nine values, Organ and his team realized that there was some overlap and that some were not as relevant as others. "During the refresh we found that several things that we thought were values were not—they were more like behavioral traits." The four values they settled on—the cornerstone of Influitive's ability to build a great culture and exceptional team—are:

1. *Take the high road,* which is all about integrity. We sleep well at night because we do the right thing and are proud of our decisions.
2. *Care like an owner,* which is about managing the long-term health of the business and the people in the business. There is more to life than our professional lives.
3. *Find a better way* that reflects innovation in everything that we do, not just in our products. We pride ourselves in bringing solutions to the table, not just problems or complaints.
4. *Win as a team.* That means we put team health over individual glory.

Organ learned from his past mistakes and started working on Influitive's culture early in the process of building the company. He also recognized over time that the initial list of values needed work. Companies often spend too much time trying to perfect their first set of values. I recommend to my clients that they approach the first set of values as a starting point and that they are a work in progress. Create a list of values that is good enough and then analyze and review which of the values are being lived and which aren't after the first three months. As I will detail later in the book, it is essential to continue to evaluate the suitability of your values periodically.

6. Skimlinks

Some executives seem to have an innate understanding of the importance of developing a strong company culture and have an intuitive sense for how it should be done. Alicia Navarro, President and cofounder of Skimlinks, is one of those fortunate executives. "From the very beginning of the business I believed that building a strong culture was essential. Culture is something that I am finely tuned to and have a natural affinity for developing. In the early days our culture developed organically; we didn't actually turn it into a formal program until a few years into the business." Navarro explained that it all came together around the hashtag #skimlove. "At first it was a little tongue in cheek, but over the years it became a lot more than that. '#Skimlove is about the way we treat our customers, our team members, how we celebrate technology and company achievements, and how we try to make every day challenging and fulfilling.' We started to have fun by prefacing words with 'skim,' like 'skimtern' in place of 'intern' and 'skimball' in place of 'football.' We would also celebrate new customer wins on Yammer and via email with the #skimlove hashtag. Then my cofounder Joe came up with the idea of putting #skimlove in neon lights in the kitchen when we moved into our first dedicated office space. #Skimlove developed into the core of our cultural DNA, describing and highlighting the fun, the camaraderie, and the love for the company and the Skimlinks family."

Navarro and her team crafted the values around the hashtag S.K.I.M.L.O.V.E., making them resonate with the team and easy to remember.

1. *Sparkle:* We have a sparkle in our eye; we're unique, quirky, and playful folk.
2. *Kickass:* We're talented, smart, capable, and great at what we do.
3. *Inventive:* We're solution-minded and work well together to solve tricky issues.
4. *Master of our domain:* We are the CEO of our personal domains; we are accountable and delivery focused.
5. *Likeable:* We're charming, fun, and interesting people who love to deliver for our customers and celebrate success.

6. *Open-minded:* We welcome difference and diversity; we can be cheeky, too!
7. *Vocal:* We are feisty, have opinions, and are confident to share them.
8. *Entrepreneurial:* We are aspiring entrepreneurs.

In his book *Built to Last,* Jim Collins writes that a key ingredient for the development of a strong culture is the construction of a unique language describing what the company does and how it operates. Creating language that is unique to the company has the effect of strengthening the bonds between the team members and setting them apart from those outside the organization. Creating values that spell out a memorable or relevant word makes them easier to remember, and in Skimlinks' case enhances the impact of the unique language the company created.

7. Periscope Data

Some companies have a handful of values; other companies find it necessary to have a longer list of values, which if used properly, can work well. The challenge with a list of eight or ten values is that they are harder for the team to remember and thus harder to implement. However, at the end of the day the number of values doesn't matter so long as they are understood, incorporated into the business, and lived by the team on a daily basis. Some companies that have an extended list of values decide to focus their efforts on a subset of the values. San Francisco-based Periscope Data is a good example of this. Melanie Tantingco is the Regional VP of People Operations for the company, which has developed a software platform that gives data professionals full control over the analytics lifecycle and non-technical users the ability to drill down into the data to quickly answer questions. The company has been recognized as a "Best Place to Work," is a top-ranked company by Comparably in 15+ categories and has been named the No. 1 "Best SaaS Product for BI and Analytics" by the SaaS Awards.

Periscope Data has eight values, and Tantingco explains some of the advantages and challenges of having that many. "The reality is that having eight values allows us to cast the widest net in terms of the types of people we hire. To work here, you don't need to align perfectly with all eight, but you do need to feel really strongly about most of them. It's worth noting that we are very purposeful around the first three values: kindness, positivity and inclusion. Those are far and away the most influential values." Tantingco has tried to shorten the list, but said, "I've had push back every time I've tried to eliminate one of the values because people have such strong feelings one way or the other about which ones we should keep."

Periscope Data's values are:

1. *We Are Kind:* We treat everyone with respect. We know that all of our teammates, customers and partners are good people.
2. *We Are Positive:* We focus on positive outcomes and solutions. We always believe our peers and teammates have the best intentions.
3. *We Are Inclusive:* We strive to make everyone feel welcome at Periscope Data. We intentionally build diverse teams to create better outcomes for our company and our community.
4. *We Are Helpful:* We take time to help our teammates, customers and partners. We know that by helping each other when needed, we all achieve our shared goals.
5. *We Are Fast:* We believe that a good decision today is better than a perfect decision tomorrow. We know that it's OK to make mistakes as long as we move fast to correct them.
6. *We Are Transparent:* We know our teammates make better decisions when they can see the full picture.
7. *We Are Data-Driven:* We make decisions with data. We believe in the power of data-informed cultures to create positive outcomes.
8. *We Are Customer-Focused:* Our work's purpose is to help our customers become successful. We always put our customers first.

By prioritizing the values of being kind, positive and inclusive, Periscope Data's leadership can look for those behaviors in the people they hire. Demonstrating kindness, positivity and inclusivity during the initial stages of the interview process gets a candidate in the door, and the hiring team can then spend more time with those better-suited candidates, exploring how well they match against the other five values. This two-tiered approach has the advantage of quickly sifting out the people who clearly don't fit the three influential values and allows the hiring team to focus on people they know have the potential to be a good fit with the company.

8. Emarsys

Ohad Hecht, CEO of Emarsys, a provider of marketing software that enables true, one-to-one interactions between marketers and consumers, formed a team to define the values of his 500-person company. "The first thing I did was create a committee. In every company you have people who have softer skills, people for whom relationships, EQ, and culture are more important than the numbers, methodology, or process. I pulled in different people who had high EQ and who genuinely wanted to help evolve the culture, telling them we needed to revisit and refine the culture." Hecht created a 10 member committee from different seniority levels and departments—contributors, managers, and leadership. "There was good support and a lot of excitement, but there was also some healthy scepticism too. Not everyone thought that what we were doing was necessary, but as the leader it's crucial to push forward if you believe in something, and I am a huge believer in the value of a strong company culture."

The committee created a culture survey and a presentation about the vision, mission, and values and circulated it to the 500 or so people in the company for their feedback. Hecht backed up the work they were doing on the committee by sending weekly emails to the team about the culture. "I wrote about the importance of the team defining the culture and that the culture and values are not just what I believe in; they're relevant to everyone in the company. I explained why we needed to look at our culture by giving examples of what we, as a company, believed to be right, and juxtaposing our beliefs with the actual behaviors we were seeing inside the company." By giving examples of the wrong behaviors, Hecht was able to demonstrate that there was a gap between the actual values of the company and the aspirational values—essentially where they wanted to be—and that had a marked impact on the company. "My emails put the company culture on people's agenda and gave me an ongoing opportunity to communicate about what we believed to be right from a culture perspective and what we were doing about it."

With a 78 percent response rate, the survey gave the committee clarity on what mattered to their people, and about 22 different values were highlighted as significant. "The committee reviewed the values and started to narrow down to the core values. We realized that 10 was probably too many—people wouldn't remember them—but if we narrowed the list down too far it might not represent what we believed in. We really thought about it. What is a value? What does it mean? How do we want people to make decisions and adopt specific behaviors for those values? We thought about examples of where those values were being lived in the company." The committee eventually decided on six core values.

1. *We are one:* We succeed together, and we work together as one team to solve challenges. We communicate openly and directly; we confront and overcome problems rather than ignoring them.

2. *We are passionate:* We believe in what we do, we take a firm opinion on what we believe is right, and we ensure that our passion is directed toward creating value for our customers.

3. *We never settle:* We do not settle for OK or good, we want great, we want the best. We do not cut corners but work to guarantee great delivery of every product.

4. *We love customers:* Customers are our lifeblood, the reason for our existence. There's nothing better than having a happy customer, and nothing worse than a dissatisfied one.

5. *We always innovate:* We think outside the box. From products to processes, procedures to our physical space, and in all walks of life. This applies not only to management, but to every individual, to initiate, strive to innovate, and improve by developing creative ideas into revolutionary results.

6. *We embrace tomorrow:* We need to be faster, better, and change at a pace quicker than our industry. We cease to exist when we stop evolving and embracing change as the opportunity it is.

IN CONCLUSION...

Defining the vision, mission and values of the company helps to bring the invisible and intangible aspects of company culture to the surface. It's the first step to helping your team understand what's important to the company, what it stands for, and what's expected of them and their colleagues in pursuit of the business goals.

Your vision, mission and values statements are powerful weapons when it comes to competing for talent. You may not be able to compete on salary and bonus, but we know that for most people, salary is not the main reason someone joins a company. Instead, you can change the conversation from being all about money to talking about the candidate's fit with the values and ability to fulfill their potential at your company. You can pull out your list of values and explain why you and the team feel that they are such a good match for what you are building and are so excited about them joining. You can also talk about how they can have a real impact on the world by joining you on the journey to fulfilling the company's vision and mission, rather than just being a tiny cog in the Facebook or Google machine.

Investing properly in defining your culture will emerge as one of the wisest steps you can take in cultivating a healthy, sustainable business. The sooner you do it the better. There is no ideal time here, but the later in the lifecycle of your business you do it, the harder it gets. Your business is at a significant disadvantage if you get to the scaling stage and you haven't yet become deliberate about developing your culture. It is almost impossible to scale right and consistently hire the tens or hundreds of people you need who also genuinely fit the values, mission and vision of the company. When you scale without a well-defined culture in place, it basically means you're risking poisoning your most valuable asset.

Most of the companies described in this chapter looked to define their vision, mission and values early on, but went through different processes to achieve their goals. Some of the key lessons shared include:

- Don't decide on your culture on your own, involve your team as early as possible in the process.
- Start the culture definition process with the vision statement. Spell it out for everyone to see, even if it feels like the fluffy useless bit.
- Develop a clear mission that will give people clarity of what the company does, who it does it for, and how this helps that client. This translates the vision into everyday actions. Write up what is critical to you in operating the business. These will be your core values, the guiding principles of the company.
- Be explicit about your values and what they mean; review them periodically; and if you can, develop an acronym that will make them easier to remember.
- Write down core values for your company as early as you can, recognizing that they can change, but should not change very often.
- Create a unique company language that uses your name or a key value, which can help develop bonds within the company, reinforce your values, and create fun in the process.
- Create a culture squad or committee who genuinely want to help develop your values and evolve the culture.

they even apply for a position. Communicating your culture during the pandemic is essential now because without an office you can't communicate the vibe or how your team operates in the same way. If your office had all the bells and whistles, or even if it didn't, candidates are not going to get the same "feeling" about the company doing Zoom calls as they would have done walking into your office.

In this and the following two chapters I look at the hiring process, which I have divided into The Funnel, The Interview and Onboarding, Probation, Performance Evaluation and Exit. One of the ways you can destroy your culture is by allowing the wrong people onto the team. You must look at the hiring process holistically to ensure you get employee attraction, acquisition and retention right. The entire hiring process needs to be optimized to communicate your culture and values, giving the candidate an authentic experience through a consistent message.

In the examples in this chapter I examine how SalesLoft does an exceptional job of communicating its culture through its website and how Periscope Data and Duel.Tech attract the right candidates through the way their job ads are written. I also explore how Runway East uses individual employee LinkedIn profiles to communicate its values, and how LiveRamp lives the values during the interview process.

YOUR CULTURE SHOULD BE ON YOUR WEBSITE

Before the coronavirus pandemic, most companies could communicate their culture through face-to-face interviews at their offices. The culture may have been undefined, yet the interaction with the interviewers, the office design, the buzz and the energy helped to convince candidates that they would probably enjoy working for the company. That luxury is no longer available in the work from home paradigm where interviews will have to be conducted via Zoom or Skype. Video conference calls are not nearly as effective as face-to-face interviews, which is why fully remote companies like Hotjar have developed lengthy, multi-stage interviews to ensure that they hire the right people and that those people can operate in their culture. Once we have come through this crisis, startups and most companies without a strong employee brand are going to have to work harder and adapt their hiring processes to convince potential employees that they should consider joining their company. Once you've defined it, one way to do that is to communicate about your culture, and demonstrate it in action, at every opportunity.

Communicating company culture has often been completely overlooked or consisted of a token paragraph or two, added without much thought to the company careers page. Looking at company websites you quickly realize that most leaders don't spend much time thinking about how people perceive their culture outside of their bubble. This approach is dangerous because people are increasingly making decisions explicitly on whether to do business with you or work for you, based on your culture and what the company stands for.

A company's website does many things, such as:

- Provide an instant first impression to first-time visitors who might become future customers.
- Convey the company's brand, product, and services, as well as information about what the company does, and, if they have paid some attention to their culture, why they do it.
- For repeat visitors, provide a place to read, watch or listen to that company's newly published content on their blog, vlog or podcast.

But there is a function a website plays that I think is all too often overlooked: forging a connection with potential employees and communicating the culture in a clear, focused and deliberate way. When people are looking for their next place to work, a company's website is something that they will typically spend anything from a few minutes to many hours looking at, as they try to get a sense of what it's like to work there and whether they will fit with the culture and vice versa. Therefore, it is naïve at best, and dangerous at worst, to overlook the role a company's website plays in communicating its culture to the outside world. A poorly communicated culture attracts the wrong talent, and it can deter the A-players who are exactly the kind of people you are trying to recruit.

Often approached as little more than a tick-box exercise, you typically only see basic information on the careers page, with little creativity or thought given to conveying the culture across the website.

To the software engineer seeking a new position, this would be quite a disappointment. To your competition this is an opportunity to differentiate against you.

By paying attention to how you convey your culture online you can give a company the "X factor" that will make it truly stand out from the crowd. SalesLoft, a sales acceleration and customer engagement platform headquartered in Atlanta, does an excellent job of communicating its culture via its website. Consider how your company's website compares when reviewing the copy and images that follow.

1. SalesLoft

As you can see in Figure 4.1 below, both the image and the copy of the main company page say something about the culture at SalesLoft. First, the photo: who wouldn't want to work with such a friendly looking group of people? The photo, along with the tagline "Engage with Integrity" and the paragraph, does a great job of telling a potential employee what the company does while also giving some insight into *how* it does it. The line toward the bottom of the page, "We're here to help you connect with customers on their terms," sets the expectation that the potential employee and the customer are both vital to the company.

Figure 4.1: Company Page

SalesLoft is the leader in sales engagement. We help brands deliver value and create trust by connecting authentically and meaningfully with their customers. We're here to help you connect with customers on their terms.

You can tell from the copy on the page in Figure 4.2 that the company has done some deep work on its values. It communicates that values are what fundamentally "drive" people to do their best work, and that the values themselves have been carefully thought through. Each is expressed in three words, with an explanation of the value given from a shared perspective. You get a real sense of the company's voice and what it stands for from this page.

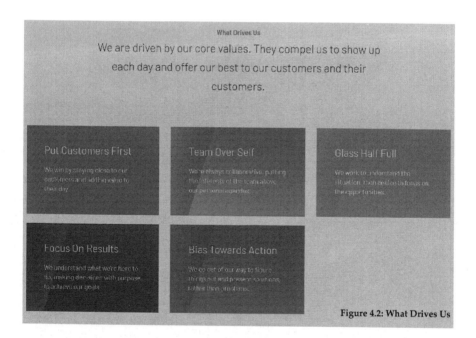

Figure 4.2: What Drives Us

The page in Figure 4.3 is another great blend of image and copy, this time showing a group of female SalesLoft employees, potentially showing that the company has its eye on the ball when it comes to diversity and inclusion and providing opportunities for women to develop and lead. The deceptively simple promise made here, that "you'll grow more here than you would anywhere else," tells the potential employee a lot about the culture and experience of working here.

We see the best in you.

You're smart, talented, and driven. At SalesLoft, you'll work with an amazing team you can learn from and teach. And we promise that you'll grow more here than you would anywhere else.

View Openings

Figure 4.3: You'll Grow More Here

Some companies tick the Corporate Social Responsibility box because it's just something that's done; others live and breathe a culture where philanthropy and giving are at its heart. SalesLoft, as seen in Figure 4.4, appears to fall into the latter category. As with their evidently deep work on values, it's clear that SalesLoft's leadership has thought deeply about philanthropy and has worked hard to understand what it means to them: the fact that they pay it forward to the local community in Atlanta attests to this, as does the section explaining that they donate more than just money. To a prospective employee who wants to work for a company that is doing good in the world, this part of the website could make SalesLoft a dream employer.

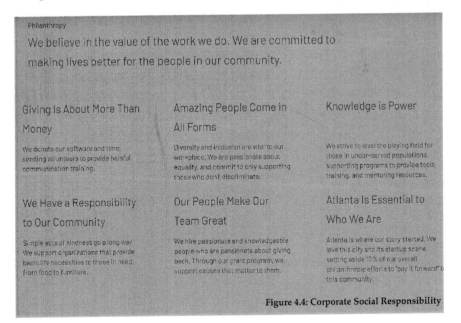

Philanthropy

We believe in the value of the work we do. We are committed to making lives better for the people in our community.

Giving Is About More Than Money

We donate our software and time, sending volunteers to provide helpful communication training.

Amazing People Come in All Forms

Diversity and inclusion are vital to our workplace. We are passionate about equality, and commit to only supporting those who don't discriminate.

Knowledge is Power

We strive to level the playing field for those in under-served populations, supporting programs to provide tools, training, and mentoring resources.

We Have a Responsibility to Our Community

Simple acts of kindness go a long way. We support organizations that provide basic life necessities to those in need, from food to furniture.

Our People Make Our Team Great

We hire passionate and knowledgeable people who are passionate about giving back. Through our grant program, we support causes that matter to them.

Atlanta Is Essential to Who We Are

Atlanta is where our story started. We love this city and its startup scene, setting aside 10% of our overall philanthropic efforts to "pay it forward" to this community.

Figure 4.4: Corporate Social Responsibility

The photos in Figure 4.5 really give the feel of what it's like to work in this company: employees receive huge cakes celebrating their "Loftiversaries," there are days where people dress up in unicorn onesies, and there are evidently lots of close relationships. The photos look natural, and people's engagement with their colleagues looks authentic. Because of this, the #1 Best Place To Work award doesn't feel cheesy or forced; it looks real and believable, fully deserving the center spot in the montage.

Figure 4.5: Showing the Company Culture

It takes a certain boldness to consistently tell potential employees that a job with this company will be "the best job you've ever had," but there is something about it that rings true on the SalesLoft website. The callout in Figure 4.6 is simple: "You could work anywhere you want," but the employees at SalesLoft want to work there because the company cares about helping you "become the best version of yourself." If you apply to work at SalesLoft, you'll get the chance to do brilliant work and become a better person. The offer is pretty compelling.

Figure 4.6: The Best Job You've Ever Had

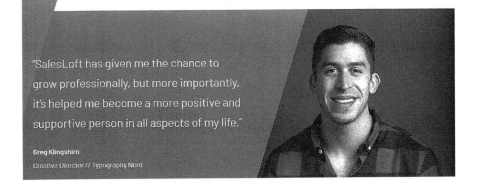

Find the best job you've ever had.

You're smart, talented, and driven. You could work anywhere you want. You choose SalesLoft because at SalesLoft, we want to help you become the best version of yourself through your service to others: our Customers and your Team Members.

See all job openings

"SalesLoft has given me the chance to grow professionally, but more importantly, it's helped me become a more positive and supportive person in all aspects of my life."

Greg Klingshirn
Creative Director // Typography Nerd

Awards aren't everything, but when a company holds a succession of awards like this it reflects something positive about the culture. The message to potential employees in Figure 4.7 is clear: this is not an average company. You can see the company's development as it progresses from being named an Atlanta Business Chronicle's Pacesetter from 2015-17 to being named the #1 Top Place to Work in Atlanta and one of the National Best Places to Work in 2018.

Other people think we're pretty great, too.

Here are just a few of the ways SalesLoft has been recognized as an incredible place to work.

2018
#1 Top Place To Work In Atlanta

2015, 2016, 2017
Atlanta Business Chronicle's Pacesetter

2017
Deloitte Fast 500's 7th Fastest Growing Company

2017
One of Georgia's Top 10 Most Innovative Companies, Georgia Technology Summit

2018
National Best Places To Work

Figure 4.7: Company Recognition

The benefits and perks in Figure 4.8 show a comprehensive and thoughtful range of employee benefits that consider all sorts of personalities, lifestyle choices, and ways of working. It is clear that SalesLoft is a high trust culture, offering unlimited vacation and stating from the outset that employees are trusted to get their work done. As with the work on values, it's clear that a lot of thought has gone into the "why" behind each benefit and perk, which the copy communicates clearly.

Figure 4.8: Benefits and Perks

Figure 4.8: Benefits and Perks Continued

3. Untracked PTO
We trust you to get your work done and be a responsible team member.

You aren't limited to a certain number of vacation days. We know you work hard, enjoy your leisure time as well.

4. Flexible Work Hours
Work life balance isn't just lip service.

Work during times that work for you. We expect you to align with your supervisor on ways you can get your work done while also meeting your personal needs.

5. Catered Lunch
Enjoy full lunches three days a week.

Meet with the entire team over lunch Monday, Tuesday, and Wednesday for varied lunches, including vegan options. You'll also enjoy a kitchen fully stocked with snacks and drinks each and every day.

6. Improve Your Commute
Make getting to work as easy as possible.

Choose either free parking at Regions Plaza or pre-paid MARTA transit to and from the office. Walk to work? You get paid for that too.

7. Casual Attire
Be comfortable at work.

We know you're a professional, let your behavior reflect this. Leave your dress attire at home if you don't have customer meetings.

8. Focus on Wellness
Mental and physical health are important.

We have a health and wellness professional on staff, offering health coaching, massage, meditation, weekly fitness classes, and more.

SalesLoft might have the most generous parental leave policy around. How many employers will pay for a newborn's diapers for a year, have meals delivered, organize and pay for your house to be cleaned? As you can see in Figure 4.9, this is clearly not just a company that has put a policy together because it had to. It is almost as if parents designed it for themselves. If you're not a parent, this won't matter to you ...but this company clearly wants to attract and retain parents and knows how to speak to them in ways that matter to them.

Figure 4.9: Parental Leave Policy

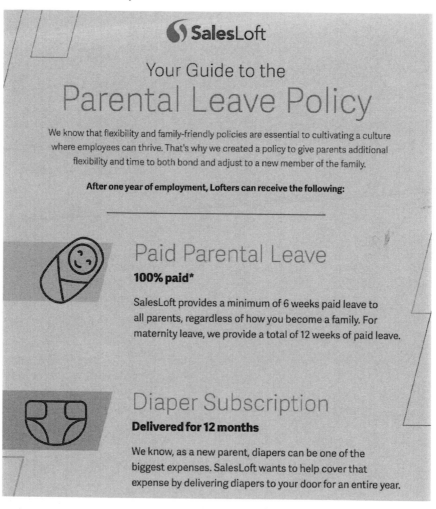

Figure 4.9: Parental Leave Policy Continued

Meal Kit Dinners for 2

Delivered twice per week for 12 weeks

No time to run to the grocery store? No problem! Salesloft will have a meal subscription service deliver meals for 2 straight to your home twice per week for 12 weeks.

Home Cleaning Service

Bi-Weekly Home Cleaning for 12 weeks

While home with a new child, SalesLoft wants you to enjoy every special moment of being a parent. Spend more time bonding with your child while having your home cleaned every-other-week for 12 weeks.

4 Week Transition Period

50% in Office, 50% Work from Home

Ease back into your work schedule with a 4-week transition period, split between home and the office.

In Figure 4.10, it's the attention to detail that makes the page so impressive. If you were going to move to Atlanta for work, you would be wondering what the city is like. Other than real estate agents, I can't think of many companies that put so much effort into answering these types of questions. SalesLoft has gone the extra mile for its applicants by providing an overview of why its city is a great place to live and work, even offering to connect new hires with colleagues who currently live within walking distance of the office to walk in with.

Figure 4.10: Learn About Atlanta

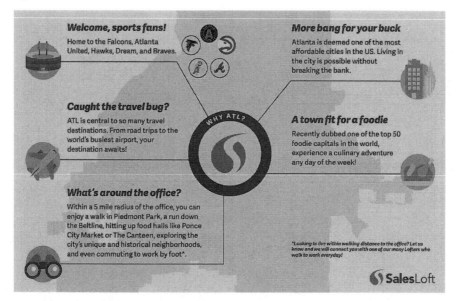

As with the other aspects of this company's culture, the attention to detail and robustness of thought is evident in how it approaches discrimination, philanthropy and grants. This tells any potential employee that this is a thoughtful, caring company that properly considers its approach to all aspects of its culture. In the middle of its clear boundaries, in Figure 4.11, is the sentence about Lofters having "huge hearts," which will appeal to the kind of people who are a good fit for SalesLoft's culture.

Figure 4.11: Giving

Non-Discrimination Policy

Any organization we partner with must not discriminate on the basis of race, religion, creed, age, gender, gender identity or expression, sexual orientation, national origin, disability, veteran status, or marital status, and they agree that they will use our grant/product/volunteer time to support projects and programs consistent with the foregoing.

Employee Solicitations

Because our Lofters have huge hearts, they often want to share their philanthropic causes with the team. We always encourage serving others, so we do not have a non-solicitation policy, but we also want to ensure a safe environment with no pressure (real or perceived) to contribute or support others' causes. Therefore, any charitable requests to teammates must take place via email, not in person, and include the disclaimer below in each request. Prior to sending to the company, all requests must first be approved by the philanthropic team, via email submission to

Grant Program

Our team members have charitable causes which are important to them, so we encourage them to apply to our grant program. The program disburses up to 25 percent of our overall philanthropic budget. Lofters apply for donations via grant applications, which are approved at a monthly meeting on a case-by-case basis by the Grant Committee. In some cases, there may be emergencies of an urgent nature, such as a natural disaster, and these will be considered on a case-by-case basis as they arise.

SalesLoft has not simply slapped some nice words and pictures on its website. The leadership has thought deeply about all aspects of their culture and has done an exceptional job getting it across to the reader. I encourage you to look at how they communicate their values and differentiate their company by exploring any of the job advertisements listed on their website[4]. Notice how the ads all start with the list of the company values, repeat them further down the ad, and then include the company's vision and mission. I particularly like how they describe what the successful candidate will achieve within one, three, six, nine, and twelve months of joining. Toward the end they reiterate the website's claim: "You will grow more here than you would anywhere else, that is a promise."

2. Duel.Tech

The classic approach to hiring involves a hastily prepared job description, often a cut-and-paste effort that invariably has very little input from the hiring manager that would differentiate it from all the other job descriptions out there. Companies hope to entice candidates to apply for a position while giving very little reason to be interested or excited about what is unique and exciting about the company. Companies that understand the importance of communicating their culture at every opportunity know that a job description is far more than a mere description. It is one of the first ways to differentiate from the ordinary and have candidates self-select in or out, encouraging vetting on both sides of the table before anyone has wasted time with telephone calls or face-to-face interviews. I've highlighted the areas in the two example job descriptions that you should focus on if you're not interested in reading the full descriptions.

Paul Archer, CEO of SaaS platform Duel.Tech, has also mastered the art of culture-centric job descriptions. Duel.Tech is a customer advocacy marketing platform that helps brands and retailers sell more by turning their customers into advocates.

The culture is showcased purposefully through the company's job descriptions. As Archer explained, "An online job advert is one of the places where a new employee interacts with our culture. It makes sense to describe our culture, our perks and include our values to inform and help attract like-minded candidates. Integrating our values into the job description allows us to give a normally bland document some personality, and really gives potential candidates a good idea of what's important to us."

Reading the job description below you will notice that Duel sounds different. It is an award-winning company that agencies "love." The founder is a record-breaking adventurer and the business is on track for substantial growth. Duel's job ad gives as much detail about the company culture and perks as it does about the role and responsibilities. *Life-first* (balance, freedom, growth, efficiency and—most importantly—happiness) as a core value goes beyond work-life balance and you get a sense from the tone of voice that the company is focused but doesn't take itself too seriously.

Duel Senior Digital and Growth Marketer (Bristol/London)

You will be responsible for managing Duel's social presence, creating, writing and managing content, PR, SEO, paid search, and paid social. In short, you will be the hero of all our online activities...

As a key employee in a dynamic startup you will have to be comfortable wearing a number of different hats, but generally you'll wear the marketing or "growth" hat, obsessively metrics-driven to bring amazing, qualified sales leads to our sales team.

You will work closely with the Founder and will directly affect the success of the business. We will build a team around you as we grow. You will also contribute ideas and additions to the product based on customer feedback.

The Business
Duel is an award-winning VC backed start-up. Our customers are global brands and marketing agencies and they love us because we help brands and retailers sell more by turning their customers into advocates.

The business was founded in Bristol by world record-breaking adventurer Paul Archer as a tool to bring adventure into people's lives, and this continues to underscore our core philosophy.

Having recently expanded into London, we are seeking ambitious, smart, and fun people to join our team in Bristol. We are on track for substantial growth over the next 12 months and require team members who can grow accordingly. The product has won a number of awards (Verizon Challenge, SXSW, Publicis90, Unilever Foundry) and we currently work with major brands and agencies.

Our Culture
- Flexible and fun, but absolutely driven to making the business a success.
- Tech and process driven.
- We work with people we like, and we like the people we work with.

- This means after work drinks, happy hours, and boozy lunches happen regularly.
- We stand by our Core Values: Life-first (balance, freedom, growth, efficiency, and—most importantly—happiness), loyalty, and ownership (responsibility, success driven, and pro-activeness).

Required
- Data and metrics driven.
- Test, iterate, test, iterate…3-5+ years' experience.
- Quantitative modeling.
- Solid organizational skills—you will be working with a CRM and need to keep perfect track of deals.
- Experience across multiple marketing and advertising channels—PPC, social, paid social, content marketing, lead generation, etc.

Nice to Have
- Total internet obsession.
- There's not a cat meme you don't know about.
- Experience creating content.
- We want to see it!
- You made something, it's out there, and you can link people to it.
- Regularly updated social media profiles.
- Excellent writing skills, with evidence to back it up.
- Ideally witty.
- Passion for technology and startups. Some experience of growth hacking.
- Advertising industry experience—working with brands, agencies, or publishers.
- Your own web presence—social media account, blog, YouTube account, etc.
- Good chat and a mischievous take on life.

What We Offer
- Open plan, busy office.

- Free tea and coffee (and beer & wine on a Friday… and most other days!).
- Flexible working hours and home working options (in fact, actively encouraged!).
- Unlimited / Zero holiday policy. If you don't need to be in the office, do the work required from anywhere in the world— Skype is a wonderful thing.
- Life-first.
- On-going training where required.
- Perks: gym membership, Headspace subscription, and work related or personal growth reading/Audible budget.
- Options scheme for all full time employees—if you help us build the company, you should own some of it!
- Bonus package.

(No recruiters please! We would rather save the money and put it toward an awesome team day out. Also no phone calls. Everything must be done by email, and if you can't follow these simple rules, we don't want to hear from you anyway. Cheers!)

3. Periscope Data

Melanie Tantingco, Regional VP People Operations, explained that at Periscope Data the hiring manager owns the hire and the fire. "I think no one has more to lose when making a hiring decision than the hiring manager, so I put a lot of accountability on the manager. A lot of HR people make a mistake by writing the job description for the manager. Why would I ever do that? I'm not the one managing them! I don't know what the expected outputs are and that's what I care about." Reviewing the company's career page and job descriptions you will notice that there's no mention about the minimum number of years' experience, because its culture is focused on output. Tantingco said, "We demonstrate the importance we place on output by having the hiring manager write a 30-, 60- and 90-day achievement plan for any new role, and this gets included in the job ad and the job description. We will not open a recruitment process until the manager completes the 30/60/90-day plan. We get tons of positive feedback from our candidates about how they love that we're already thinking about what the person will be doing one, two, and three months from now, even before they show up for their first day."

Reading the job description below you get the sense that Periscope Data has really thought about how to differentiate themselves in the competitive San Francisco market, therefore doing an excellent job of enticing potentially suitable candidates to apply. You will notice how the company's mission to turn data teams into superheroes is communicated to the reader: "Our customers love us: Many of our teammates on the product, data, and sales teams are former customers that joined to help turn data teams into superheroes."

The 30/60/90-day ramp up demonstrates that the team leader, not just HR, has thought about the role and what success will look like. The culture pitch that the job description makes is backed up by the recognition the company has received: "We've been recognized by Comparably, Glassdoor, *Bay Area News Group*, and *San Francisco Business Times* for our amazing company culture and some of the perks the company offers. We provide free lunch every day and cover healthcare for all of our employees." Here's one of their job descriptions:

Periscope Data Business Operations and Analytics Manager (San Francisco)

We're looking for inventive, full-stack data experts that are unconventionally curious, rigorous in their attention to detail, and maintain a healthy degree of scepticism. You should be technically adept and possess a keen eye for business, with a real passion for making an impact through creative storytelling and timely actions.

Why you should join our data team:

Our customers love us: Many of our teammates on the product, data, and sales teams are former customers that joined to help turn data teams into superheroes.
We help build a better product (for ourselves): In marketing, they say "Remember, you're not the target audience." But what if you were? You will help design a product targeted at you.
We are the cutting edge: We frequently provide feedback to partner vendors and contribute to open source packages. You'll have the

opportunity to participate in thought leadership, open source development, and community moderation.

Everyone on the team is full-stack: From developing data models in Airflow/DBT to delivering recommendations to senior leadership, everything is in each individual's purview.

Full exposure to all parts of the business: The data team has built cash forecasting and GAAP reporting for the finance team, pipeline tracking and health analysis for the sales team, cohort investigations for the marketing team, customer health scores for the customer success team, and feature affinity curves for the product team, just to name a few. You will partner with and be exposed to every team: an unparalleled opportunity to learn about all the nuts and bolts of a business.

How you'll ramp:

Within your first week...
> You'll learn the business from most of the key business owners, including Sales, Marketing, Finance, Support / Solutions, Product, and Engineering.

By Day 30...
> You will deftly answer questions by querying our data models and systems of record (including SFDC, Zuora, Intercom, Outreach, Bizible, etc.), while increasing the adoption of data across the company.

By Day 60...
> You will start to identify and pursue projects that directly drive revenue. You will be writing ETL scripts in SQL and Python to retrieve unstructured data from the depths of S3 and code business logic into structured data transformations. You will implement a single source of truth by updating existing models and generating new data resources from sales activity data, marketing attribution data, and customer interaction logs.

By Day 90...
> You will make recommendations that directly influence business outcomes. You will identify areas of opportunity, spin up collaborative teams, and report on successes.

About Periscope Data

- We're a passionate, venture-funded team with more than 1,000 customers, including Adobe, Flexport, EY, Uber, ZipRecruiter, Fender, Meredith & Tinder.
- We are onboarding rapidly! We've grown our team 3x over the last two years.
- We believe strongly in a data-driven approach to all that we do. We're constantly measuring and optimizing everything about the business.
- We've been recognized by Comparably, Glassdoor, *Bay Area News Group*, and *SF Business Times* for our amazing company culture.
- Our product is very sticky. Users spend ~20 hours per week doing technical analysis on our platform.
- We have super high customer retention—better than best in class SaaS companies.
- We provide free lunch every day and cover healthcare for all of our employees.
- We've recently moved into our new global headquarters, a newly renovated building in SOMA, customized to our unique needs.

This job description also does a great job of communicating several of Periscope Data's company values—from being fast, to their customer focus, and how the company is data driven.

4. Runway East

Natasha Guerra, CEO of the UK-based coworking space Runway East, ensures that the company's values and culture are easily available to anyone who wants to read about them. "Our culture is radically different to our competition because we are laser-focused on creating environments that help tech startups succeed and I believe that it is critical to communicate about it at every possible opportunity." In addition to having the culture detailed on its website and via a culture deck you can download[5], the company includes the values everywhere it can, many of them places we don't usually see. They appear in its job ads, job descriptions and in Tweets and Youtube videos. The company even encourages employees to include a brief description of the values in their personal profile on LinkedIn. Guerra told me, "It makes sense that a candidate will want to understand more about who is working at the company. We know they research our website and they search LinkedIn to get a sense of the calibre of the people in the team. Including our values, not just in our company profile page on LinkedIn, but also in the profiles of our employees reinforces the message that we are serious about living our values at Runway East. It also differentiates us from the competition." Candidates will come across the Runway East values multiple times during the recruitment process, whereas with the competition candidates will be lucky to read about the culture at all. You can understand how effective this approach can be in informing potential candidates about the company's culture and helping to attract the people who might be a good match for a company's values.

5. LiveRamp

Anneka Gupta, President and Head of Products and Platforms at LiveRamp, wants her company's values clearly demonstrated throughout the recruitment process. "We are continually thinking about how to create a great experience for our candidates during the interview process, because that's their first point of contact with us. We want the whole recruitment journey to reflect our values; if we're not reflecting our values in our recruiting process, then why would the candidate believe that any of the values that we say are true for the company are actually true?" Gupta joined the company straight out of Stanford University and having only ever worked at LiveRamp, she had never come across any of the negative experiences that candidates have when interviewing at other companies. So, she asked her friends to tell her their stories and was horrified to hear that some companies wait three weeks to get back to people, or never get back to people at all. "We are determined to get back to all applicants within 24 hours of application, so when someone applies, we either tell them immediately that we don't have a role for them, or put them through to the next stage of the interview process straightaway. Candidates tell us they appreciate the speed, even if we don't progress with them. One of the advantages of this strategy is the goodwill it builds in the ecosystem." By responding to candidates in this way LiveRamp is demonstrating two of their values in action: *We respect people and respect time* and *We get stuff done.*

IN CONCLUSION...

It is crucial to recognize that the hiring process starts long before the actual interview stage and you need to be communicating about your culture at every opportunity. By making your values and culture available and easily understood you align more closely with your ideal prospective employees and deter the unsuitable candidates from even starting the interview process. Your company values should be apparent at every step of the process, beginning when a potential candidate looks at your website or checks your employees' social media profiles. To showcase your culture more consistently:

- Treat your employee acquisition process like a longer funnel: the first email or phone screen is already halfway down the funnel.
- Use every step in the funnel to inform your audience, demonstrate your values in action and repeat your culture message.
- Consider how fully you can detail and integrate your company values where prospective employees and customers can see it most easily: on your website.
- Use social media sites to share your culture message.
- The hiring manager should own the job description, and it should differentiate the company from others and let potential candidates know what to expect both initially and at key moments months after starting the job.
- Give your job ads and job descriptions personality, include information about the culture and the company's vision, mission and values.

Everything you can do to communicate your company culture to prospective employees clearly will benefit both you as a company and the people considering working there. By describing who you are, what you stand for, and what you value as a company, you will make it easier for prospective hires to know if they resonate with your culture and whether they might be the right fit.

Chapter 5

Interview Process

"I'd rather interview 50 people and not hire anyone than hire the wrong person." – Jeff Bezos, Founder & CEO, Amazon

The typical interview process won't work at a culture-driven company because it focuses mainly on evaluating skills and experience. It leaves out the more in-depth discussions about the culture and the questions about whether the candidate matches the company's values. Customizing your interview processes and adapting your interviewing techniques to your company's specific needs are some of the most crucial things you can do to develop the right candidate evaluation and attraction strategy. You can't expect different or better results if you interview the same way everyone else does. Each company should have a clearly defined candidate persona and develop a disciplined recruitment process to attract and hire the right candidates. As part of this process it is critical to develop the tools and capabilities to interview candidates for *values* fit rather than *culture* fit. As I will discuss later in this chapter, it is impossible to hire for culture fit.

It is impossible to hire for culture fit

Furthermore, if you're hiring remote employees, you need to build an interview process that demonstrates whether the candidate can operate—work and communicate—the same way your team does.

You need to design an interview process that involves the candidate working and communicating with your team using the same methods and channels that your team would normally use. If you are building a hybrid work environment, you should take a remote-first approach and still interview all candidates as if they were a joining a fully remote company. As I explain in Chapter 12, this is to ensure that your people who choose to work remotely don't end up alienated and feeling like "second-class citizens" and can operate in the manner your company requires. If you design your recruiting process right, you will evaluate candidates based on their skills and experience as well as:

- Their actual ability to do the job.
- The quality of work produced.
- Their behavior during process.
- Their verbal and written communication.
- Their fit with the values of the company.

In this chapter I look at how Thread, CloudFactory, Hotjar and Lillydoo customize the typical recruitment process for their company's talent acquisition needs. I explore how ClubCollect approaches hiring for values-fit not culture-fit, and how Pardot created a Culture Check Team with veto rights on any candidate who doesn't match the culture.

1. CUSTOMIZE THE INTERVIEW PROCESS
Kieran O'Neill, cofounder and CEO of Thread, hits the nail on the head when he talks about the need to do things differently. This section discusses how Thread uses multiple tests to evaluate candidates, and how CloudFactory uses deep and thoughtful questions to whittle down the candidate pipeline early in the process. I also explore the recruitment process at Hotjar, which helps the fully remote company hire the right people without any of the team ever meeting the candidates face-to-face. Finally, I look at Lillydoo, where the founders flipped the hiring process, so that they aren't involved until a candidate is being endorsed by the team they would be working with.

1. Thread
Kieran O'Neill, CEO of Thread, says that he received a great deal of

advice and help from a friend who was a recruiter who had been involved first-hand during the early days of the company's development in the early stage hiring phase at Facebook. O'Neill turned to her frequently for advice when building out the Thread team and eventually approached her to join the company as the 17th employee. Most startups don't hire a Head of Talent as early as O'Neill did. Hiring a dedicated lead so soon exemplifies O'Neill's commitment to sourcing the best people and building a strong company culture, and not doing it the same way every other startup does. "If you follow the same hiring process as the average business, you'll be hiring the same sort of average candidates," O'Neill said. Together they designed a three-stage interview process to ensure they could recruit the best candidates.

1. Thread's hiring process starts off with a remote test that evaluates the candidate's ability to do the job. This is chiefly composed of a custom exercise or case study that's developed for every job role that the company hires for. As O'Neill explained, "We build the test in-house, and if it's a brand-new role, we ask people from outside the business, who we know are subject matter experts, to help us refine the exercise. Every candidate that we put through the process will do the bespoke exercise and we are able to rule out 80-90 percent of the original candidate pool from that exercise. We invite the ones who pass the custom exercise test to on-site interviews."

2. Next, the on-site interview and exercises are designed to evaluate the candidate's functional skills and get a sense of who they are. For each of the interviews, Thread has developed a hiring spec document that O'Neill said serves to list "what we're expecting and how good the candidate should be in each role's specifications. We take each criterion and either design standardized interview questions or create an on-site exercise around it. We believe that you can assess some things in an interview format, but that there are many areas that you can't assess

effectively." O'Neill believes that interviews are an essential part of the process but are limited in their value and are not nearly as valuable to the company as passing the range of tests they've devised as part of the hiring process. "For example, when hiring for our Head of Finance, the first round of on-site interviews actually consisted of three exercises and two interviews, with the candidate already having completed the remote exercise as well." At the end of the first round, the candidates had completed four different tests covering key areas that the Thread team was evaluating. "Our process gives a clear indication of how good the candidates actually are in these areas, whereas an interview simply shows whether people can talk about what they might have done."

3. The second on-site interview evaluates whether the candidate's values match with the company. "The interviewers score the candidates against the questions they ask and for each answer they'll give a score between 1 and 7, where 7 is excellent, 6 is very good, 5 is good, and so on. Together with the score the interviewer indicates his/her confidence in the score." Thread has a minimum score of five out of seven for all the values. "We don't expect perfection everywhere, but less than five is serious; we'd have a conversation about how much we could realistically coach the candidate on that value. It's definitely a no if they score below 5 on multiple values."

2. CloudFactory

CloudFactory, the human-powered data processing for artificial intelligence and automation company, has offices in Nepal, the UK and Kenya and runs a hybrid work model. The company's online recruitment application process's initial stages are focused on evaluating how much a candidate resonates with and believes in the company's mission. The online application starts with five questions, the answers to which help the company weed out candidates who aren't committed enough. They use questions that are open-ended, thoughtful and sometimes hard to answer. For example, one of the questions is, "Tell us about your story," while another is, "Do you have a purpose in life?" Joel Montgomery, VP of Culture, explained, "You can immediately tell whether someone actually put effort into their online application. You can be the most brilliant person on earth, but if you didn't put the effort into your application, I'm not interested in interviewing you, never mind having them on board." The answers from the candidates who are genuinely interested in the company and its mission—to connect 1 million people in the developing world to meaningful work, while raising them up as leaders to address poverty in their communities—stand out from the candidates who are just trying to get a job. "Our starting point is to try to use questions in the first stage of the process to eliminate the candidates who aren't interested in what we do and get a better understanding of the people prepared to invest time and effort in their application."

Montgomery recalled one memorable exchange that demonstrates how he thinks about the candidate's responses through the values-fit lens. "We had an applicant from Kenya who answered all the questions except the one about having a purpose in life, which is an optional question. In the interview I said I was curious why she skipped that question. She was open and honest and said, 'Honestly, I just really haven't figured it out yet.' I prefer that because it wouldn't help anybody if she pretended to be something she wasn't and her answer matched well with our value, 'We speak truth and life.' The CloudFactory environment is not the perfect workplace for everyone and for those who won't fit, the company wants the process to help them understand it quicker. "If we can help people realize where their best fit is, they're going to be happier. We want people who genuinely fit here and if they don't fit CloudFactory we don't want to waste their time or ours."

Both Thread and CloudFactory use online processes to filter candidates before the on-site interview stages. To extend their online interview capability to be able to operate remotely, both companies will need to redesign their processes to allow for effective online evaluation in place of the face-to-face interviews they would normally conduct. The Hotjar interview process described below is a great example of how a company that has operated as a remote organization has developed an intensive and effective online interview process from day one.

3. Hotjar

David Darmanin, cofounder and CEO of the fully remote SaaS startup Hotjar, credits his company's rapid growth and success to the team's thorough and thoughtful hiring process. When I spoke with Darmanin, the website heatmap and behavior analytics company had grown from the four founders who started the business to a team of 70, generating over $16 million in annual recurring revenue, all in under four years. The interesting challenge that the team faces when recruiting is that, as a fully remote company, the candidates are never interviewed in the flesh, so to speak. Darmanin outlined the customized five-stage process the company has developed to overcome the limitations of hiring for fully remote teams:

1. The interview process starts with an online survey. "The survey is there to eliminate people; we ask rather simplistic questions to see if we're on the same page. We design the survey questions for quick and easy no's; the key is to avoid false positives, so the questions have to be bulletproof. You have to be careful not to lead with soft questions (e.g., what tools the applicants use) because you run the risk of disqualifying people based on something that is totally learnable, but they might not currently know. The survey is there to quickly evaluate applicants' mindsets and to get a sense of their fit with our values."

2. At the next stage Hotjar asks candidates to video record their answers to five questions. "We're basically exploring whether we would want to spend a Sunday with this person at the office, if we had an office. So, for example, if we're looking to explore the candidate's honesty, we might ask: 'If you could do anything on a Monday morning,

what would you do?' If the applicant responds, 'Oh, I'd check my email and plan the week,' we'd be like: 'Yeah, I call bullshit on that!' Calling bullshit doesn't mean we're going to disqualify that person, but if they move ahead to the next stage, we will bring that up later on in the process and say: 'There's no way you'd do that on a Monday morning if you could do anything you wanted to. Come on, what would you do?' It's interesting to see the way people react to certain questions. It helps us determine if they are a good fit in terms of being honest, candid and explaining themselves on the fly. Secondly, and very importantly, at this stage we start to look at what they would bring to our culture; culture is not static, and we expect everyone who joins the company to contribute to it."

3. The third stage starts the more interactive part of the interview process and can be done via video conference or audio and explores how the candidate fits with the company's values. "At Stage 3, we put them on the spot a little bit: 'What would you do in this scenario?' The majority of the interview is focused on emotional intelligence and awareness, with questions like, 'Tell us about a conflict you've experienced.' We're still identifying red flags here. We're looking for assholes, people who would be unreasonable to work with, such as potentially racist and intolerant people. These red flags tend to come out very quickly when you start to discuss certain topics."

4. The fourth stage, which can take a couple of days, is what the company calls performance recruitment, where a two- or three-part task is designed for each role the company hires for. As Darmanin explained, "The first part of this stage is getting the candidate to look at a system, understand it, and then create a diagram for it, explain how it works, and suggest how it can be improved. We're looking at whether people can think in terms of systems and whether they are analytical and can understand and

describe something effectively." Being remote, it is critical to understand how the candidate makes sense of the task, how they process information, and how they take feedback. The task is tailored for everyone, from engineers to customer service representatives.

The second part is for the candidate to demonstrate that they can improve a process. Darmanin said, "We also ask them to think about and improve at least one thing we're actually going to use in the business; no matter how good that product or process already is, we ask them to change at least part of it, to rework it and improve it. At this stage when we give feedback we try to make it a little bit harsh or blunt, to see if the candidate can take it; can they listen, do they understand what we said, and do they go away and fix or change what they heard in the feedback?"

The last part of the task stage is a presentation to the team. "The final part of the task is when the candidate presents their work to the team; they're evaluated in the end by the hiring team, which always includes the recruitment coordinator and the hiring manager. We ask the candidate to grade their own work, which tells us if they're modest and self-aware enough to understand where they did a good job and where they did a bad job." Everyone involved in the process then votes on whether we should progress to the final stage with that process.

5. If the candidate makes it to the fifth stage, they will have a final call with Darmanin. "This is the point where I am mainly checking the quality of the hiring team's decision by doing what I call the desperation test. My key focus is to find out if the team was so desperate to fill this role that they lowered their guard somewhere. I'm also evaluating at the highest level on whether there is a values fit. I also shift my focus toward this candidate's future. For example, if they're applying for a 'customer services hero' role, I'm considering what that role might be a stepping stone to, how long they are going to be with us, and what

the real motivation is for wanting the role. If the candidate gets through the fifth stage, we offer them the role."

Hotjar has built a multi-stage recruitment process that takes longer than your average process but gives the company a 360-degree evaluation of the candidate. The company pays the candidates who get to the task stage for their work because they understand that the person will spend a significant amount of time interacting with the team and completing the task.

4. Lillydoo

Lillydoo is a subscription service baby care company that offers diapers, wipes and changing mats. The company was founded in 2015 by Gerald Kullack and Sven Bauer to bridge the gap between performance, skin-friendliness, sustainability-oriented production and unique design. The company is based in Frankfurt, employs 180 people and has revenues that have grown rapidly from €1.7 million revenue in the first year, €12 million in the second year, €40 million in the third year, to €70 million in the fourth year. Early on in the growth of the business, the founders developed a twist on the typical early founder interview mindset and process. Founders usually want to make sure that new employees fit with what they believe the right employee profile is. So, the founders conduct the first round of interviews and will involve other team members if they like a candidate. "We decided from the beginning to have the functional team that is responsible for filling the role to drive the interview process. Marketing was the first department to hire a second person onto their team, and Johanna Wielens, who was a Junior Marketing Manager at the time, reviewed all inbound applications and started interviewing the potential candidates she felt were a good fit for the role and the company." The Lillydoo founders feel that it is more significant that the team members decide what they think about the candidates first. "Anyone involved in the hiring process has full veto rights on any candidate they interview, Sven and I could of course reject a candidate we didn't believe was suitable for the role, but giving responsibility to the teams to lead the hiring from the beginning has been instrumental in helping us scale the business to where it is now."

As an aside, Wielens is an excellent example of how rapidly someone can grow and develop at a successful high-growth company like Lillydoo. As Kullack explains, "We hired Johanna as a Junior Marketing Manager and three years later she is the Vice President of Marketing and now leads a team of 30 people."

2. INTERVIEW FOR VALUES FIT, NOT CULTURE FIT

To interview for culture fit you would need to be able to describe what your company's culture is accurately and consistently. Not a single leader I have spoken with could accurately describe their culture clearly. I have talked to hundreds of founders. When asked if any of their team could describe their culture, and if they would all describe it in the same way, these leaders answered categorically, "No." This is not a surprise because culture is a random collection of good *and* bad habits, behaviors, principles, norms, assumptions and beliefs that are for the most part invisible, subconscious and intangible. Company culture, or "the way we do things around here," changes as a company grows and as I mentioned in the first chapter, the way your company operates when there are eight people in the team is vastly different from the way you work when there are 50 of you. The team of 50 requires more management, structure and process, budgets and different communication patterns. A typical high-growth company will also include investors, board members and shareholders who need to be managed. The way your business operates when your business has expanded to 500 employees on three continents across multiple time zones is completely different again. Your company culture is also constantly changing in response to the external factors impacting the business: another reason why it is impossible to hire effectively for culture fit. What leaders actually do when they claim to hire for culture fit is more like a high-level "gut instinct" approach to recruitment, which is biased, unreliable and unscalable.

So, how do we create an interview process that evaluates whether a candidate "fits" with a company and is less reliant on our gut instinct, less biased, more reliable and scalable?

The answer is simpler than you might think: values-based hiring. This means hiring people based on the fact that they can do the job and that their personal values fit with the company's values. You can teach a person a new skill, but you can't easily change a person's character or value. Well-defined core values don't often change, if at all, so if a candidate's values fit with the company today, it's very likely that they will still fit in 6-, 12- or 36-months' time.

Many companies come up with a list of values and make the mistake of sticking them up on a poster on the wall hoping that somehow their people will just automatically "live" them. Many branding agencies will help you define your mission, vision, purpose and values. The best way to think about using a brand agency to define your culture is to buy a sports car without an engine. It looks pretty but it is completely useless.

The main problem with most values is that they are open to interpretation. Different people can and do interpret the same words in different ways. Take the word "teamwork," for example. One person's interpretation of teamwork could be a group of people working together to achieve a common goal. Another person's interpretation might be that the team always comes first before any individual's agenda. Neither is wrong, but you can see that these different interpretations of what teamwork means might end up with one team member making a different decision than another when faced with the same situation. Often, the interpretation and decision that is made suits the person's individual needs making the decision and is not in the company's best interests. This happens all the time and is one of the reasons why people doubt the effectiveness of defining company values. Another problem, which we will cover later in the book, is knowing what to do with your values once you've defined them.

As you will see in this section, values are associated with a set of clearly related expected behaviors when defined correctly. As the phrase suggests, expected behaviors are the behaviors your company expects to see lived by *everyone* on the team as they do their jobs.

This section discusses Pardot's values-based interview questions which, to an interviewee, simply sound like normal interview questions, but they actually explore how a candidate fits with the company values of being positive, self-starting and supportive. I go into detail about how ClubCollect created their values-based interview questions by extracting a list of the expected behaviors they associate with each value.

1. Pardot

David Cummings, founder of Atlanta Tech Village, explained that his company developed specific interview questions exploring the candidate's fit using the values from his former company, Pardot: being positive, self-starting and supportive. "We developed a series of interview questions that assessed for values fit, but which, to the interviewee, simply sounded like a normal interview question. The person on the receiving end didn't know that we were asking specifically to test their fit with our core values." The company also developed a Culture Check Team to help as the company started growing rapidly. "We decided to create cross-functional teams made up of two people from different departments. They were chosen because they really embodied our values and received training to assess candidates solely for values fit and to test them on how they would behave to demonstrate that fit. By the time we sold Pardot, we had three two-person Culture Check Teams in place and one of those teams would interview every candidate who had made it through to the last stage of the process. The Culture Check Teams could veto anybody out if they didn't match the values."

2. ClubCollect

Adam Posma is the founder and Chairman of ClubCollect, an Amsterdam-based SaaS billing and payments platform for non-professional sports clubs. Posma and the ClubCollect management team developed their values-based interview process by taking the company's core values and extracting a list of the expected behaviors they associated with each value. They did this by asking themselves what each value means to them and how does it, or should it, translate into their actual everyday behaviors inside the company. Once the expected behaviors had been defined, the management team then sat down and created a list of interview questions based on those expected behaviors.

According to Posma, "The advantage of this values-based hiring process is that each candidate is asked the same list of behavior-based questions to evaluate their fit with the company's values. We score each candidate's answer from 1 to 7 for vividness and believability, and the candidate who scores the highest total for all questions emerges as the person most aligned with our company's core values.

It has turned recruiting for values fit into a data-driven process. More importantly, it helps to dilute any 'similar to me' hiring bias and everyone in the company can learn to do it." Posma explained how companies like ClubCollect create values-based interview questions.

1. "We came up with a list of company values that the team resonated with and cared about. The list contained a combination of values that we were living and values that we aspired to live by." Posma and his team reviewed the values to ensure that they were achievable by everyone in the company and that everybody felt that they were relevant and realistic, not just wishful thinking.

2. Behaviors have the advantage of being specific, defined, demonstrable, can be trained for, and are visible in action and therefore measurable and manageable. Posma explained, "We then defined a list of expected behaviors we would expect to see associated with each value by asking ourselves, 'What does this value mean to us and how does that, or how should that, translate into the behaviors we expect from one another inside the company?' An example of a ClubCollect's value and related expected behavior is: Develop yourself and grow the company: We translate challenges and problems into opportunities to grow and develop. Another simple process to extract the expected behaviors from a value is to look at the dictionary definition and then think about the verbs and actions you would associate with the value. Also consider the value in relation to what you do in the company currently and that you would like to see more of."

3. "We then turned those expected behaviors into interview questions. For example, for our company value: Impress the customer, we defined the expected behavior: We find solutions to problems and act to solve those problems for our customers. We developed a database of interview

questions with specific questions for each role. The sales leader examples:

- Which customer, if I called them now, would be most impressed with your ability to solve hard problems and why?
- Can you give me an example of a problematic customer situation that looked insurmountable from the outset, but you managed to overcome?
- Give me an example where your company made a strategic decision that either did or could negatively impact a large customer and how you solved this problem.

Examples of the interview questions we developed for a product leader role are:

- Talk in detail about how you have overcome poor customer feedback that was unexpected.
- Explain how you handled the situation where one executive believed that Feature A was more important, and another executive believed Feature B was more important.
- Can you give me an example of where you have had to cut corners to get the product launched? What did you cut and why? How did it impact the user?"

4. Using a behavior-focused approach to evaluate values fit allows the interviewer to dig deeper and understand the root cause of that behavior. The interview technique Posma uses includes:

- Looking for the candidate to describe in detail the situation they were in, what their thought process was, and what they did to take advantage of the situation or solve the problem.
- Exploring the answers given by asking follow-up questions to understand:
  - What were the circumstances?
  - What was at stake?

- Why did the candidate behave the way they did?
- How they could have behaved differently?
- What were the underlying drivers?
- What was the impact?
- What did candidate learn?
- How does the candidate's behavior and approach match with the company's?

- Using the Five Whys technique to explore the cause-and-effect relationships of the candidate's answer.

"We ensure that two people conduct the values stage interview. One asks more questions and watches the candidate, while the other takes written notes of their impression of the candidate and their response to those questions. Both candidates score the candidate's answers. In this way we try to ensure that we get a balanced evaluation of the candidate." Posma went on to explain the advantages of the values-based interview approach, "By asking each candidate the same set of behavior-focused questions we create consistency across the values evaluation interview process. By scoring the candidate's answers for vividness and believability, we've created a standardized evaluation method for each candidate that mitigates the need for gut instinct. The other advantage is this process is highly scalable as anyone on the team can learn to do this."

IN CONCLUSION...

The interview is such a key part of the hiring process that it makes sense to invest time in designing one that fits the company's needs. Doing what everyone else does is lazy; it fails to do your company justice, and it doesn't differentiate your business. The interview should eliminate the unsuitable candidates early in the process. A well thought out and well-run interview process is an opportunity for you to demonstrate your values and behaviors in action and ultimately why the right candidate should want to join your company.

Some options to consider include:

- Treat the hiring process as a multi-layered, multi-channel strategy.

- Design questions for the first online candidate evaluation stage that allows the candidates to demonstrate their interest in, and commitment to, fulfilling the company's vision and mission.
- Create interview tasks that correspond to your business's challenges or opportunities and encourage the candidate to work with your team as they complete the task.
- Create a database of values-based interview questions.
- Give everyone in the interview process veto rights to allow for early termination of the process or open up the discussion for a candidate's fit at the company.
- Create a Culture Check team to be the final arbiter of the candidate's fit with the company's values.

Chapter 6

Onboarding, Probation, Performance Evaluation and Exit

"We want to focus on creating a memorable experience for the new hire in the first year rather than processing them in the first few weeks."
– Cheryl Hughey, Director of Onboarding, Southwest Airlines

After a new employee has signed the offer letter and the employment agreement, there is a window of opportunity to ensure that the time and money invested in attracting that person was not in vain. This is a unique period in time, both for your company and the person joining. The new joiner is untainted by the business's realities and the good and bad aspects of your culture. You will never have this greenfield opportunity with them ever again. The employee wants to contribute, demonstrate their capabilities and become a valued member of the organization. The company wants to quickly and efficiently integrate a highly productive employee who will add to the business and the bottom line. You have a better chance of integrating a committed, engaged and valuable employee for the company if you invest in designing effective post-interview processes that integrate and demonstrate your culture, and how you live the values, mission and vision. In this chapter, I will look into how culture-driven companies approach onboarding, probation and performance evaluation and exit interviews.

ONBOARDING

A lot of companies miss a massive opportunity by treating employee onboarding as an afterthought and if the process is optimized at all, it is for the wrong goal of getting a new employee to be productive as soon as possible. Leadership fails to understand that the onboarding process plays a critical role in the success of any new hire. Onboarding is a decisive step toward integrating the new person into the company's culture, which, in the long run, is more important than extracting value from the new hire as quickly as possible. Leaders who don't have a well-designed onboarding process and treat employee onboarding as "not that critical," are essentially leaving new employees to fend for themselves. In an office situation, this could impede their ability to become a culturally integrated, happy, efficient, effective worker who achieves the desired outcomes. In a remote working environment, this approach to onboarding is nothing short of insane.

You need to document the onboarding process in a remote working environment. In an office-based environment, the new joiner would lean across their desk and ask for clarification on how things are done or watch how other team members behave. The experience of walking the new joiner around the office to introduce them to people and sitting down with them for lunch is impossible to replicate in a remote work environment. Over time, the new joiner would learn by osmosis about the way the company operates and solves problems, and gets a sense of the underlying currents of the company's culture, from what they saw happening in the office. For a productive remote onboarding session, it is essential to:

- Start the onboarding process before the new joiner's first day.
- Create a communication cadence that may look something like this:
  – Communication starts 30 days before with different communication events that happen 15 days, 5 days, 3 days, 2 days and 1 day before they join.
  – Then follow up 1 day, 2 days, 3 days, 4 days, 5 days, 15 days, 30 days and 60 days after their joining.
- Schedule the necessary meetings.
- Check in with the new joiner twice per day for the first few days.
- Have an onboarding FAQ as well as a document detailing your culture.

- Arrange a buddy/mentor for the first month (at least).
- Agree on their goals for 3/6/12 months.
- Introduce the new joiner to any relevant subject matter groups.
- Adapt for Zoom-fatigue:
  – Limit video calls to 45 minutes with decompression time.
  – Spread onboarding out over a longer period.
  – Balance learning and thinking time.
- Give the new joiner tasks or projects with multiple team interaction points to work on for quick wins.
- Get an understanding of their feedback preferences – how they like to give and receive feedback.

The keys to developing a successful onboarding program:
- Eliminate anxiety from the process.
- Develop trust and build relationships within the company.
- Help them to understand the invisible currents of "the way we work around here."
- Allow them to demonstrate their strengths quickly.
- Create an environment where they can feel safe enough to be themselves.

Amanda Lannert, the CEO of Jellyvision, a software company that helps employees pick health insurance and other benefits, aptly described a new joiner's state of mind, "At the end of your first day you have probably come from the height of your power at your last job to the bottom of your power at Jellyvision. You're tired, anxious, emotionally exhausted, and you're completely confused."

The companies I highlight in this section all do the onboarding basics well: explaining how the company operates, what the core tools are, what the culture is, introducing new joiners to the team and setting up the necessary meetings to start building relationships across the company. This section discusses how even before starting their new job, new joiners at Influitive feel like they're already part of the team. CharlieHR uses the buddy system to make sure that new team members get up to speed quickly. To demonstrate trust Hotjar sends new employees a welcome package that includes a company credit card. At BorrowMyDoggy they ask all new employees to work in the customer service department before they start their actual role. Jellyvision uses two standing ovations to welcome new employees to the company. Thread creates a Development Plan for each new employee based on feedback given during their interview process. Headliner makes every new joiner responsible for improving the onboarding process for the next intake. By rotating the onboarding location between their offices, Emarsys allows new employees from other countries to absorb local office culture. And Next Jump works on emotional and character development with new hires by injecting stress early into the onboarding process.

1. Influitive

At Influitive, a marketing advocacy software platform, onboarding begins before the candidate starts work—it begins when they accept the offer. As outlined by founder and Executive Chairman Mark Organ, "We send the candidate a package in the mail with some reading material and company branded clothing. There can be a couple of months between accepting the offer and joining the company, so we will invite them to our town hall meetings and any parties or events that are happening before they have formally joined, for them to feel like they're already part of the team. The first week in the job is planned out for them; depending on their seniority level, they will do job shadowing and have meetings set up with the relevant people."

2. CharlieHR

CharlieHR is an HR platform for small businesses that automates the administrative headaches of running a company so that management "can focus on building real value." Founder and Chairman Rob O'Donovan believes in demonstrating the values match between the new employee and the company as soon as possible. O'Donovan explained that "A new joiner is partnered with a buddy from the team, and it's the buddy's responsibility to make sure that the new joiner gets up to speed quickly, is integrating well, is having a good time and understands what PACT (the acronym for the company's four values: *Passion, Ambition, Curiosity* and *Together*) stands for. Every new joiner has to do a 'PACTivity presentation,' describing how they relate to PACT, and showcasing how they resonate with one or more company values." Encouraging such value-centric activities is "a powerful way to show the new joiner how much we care for and live our values and immediately builds a bond between the new joiner and the team."

3. Hotjar

David Darmanin, CEO of Hotjar, said, "Before a new employee joins, they receive a welcome pack with their Kindle, headset, the *StrengthsFinder* book and their company credit card." The founders decided early on to trust in their people by allowing them to have budgets and allowances that they control. New hires get a strong indicator of this trust when they receive a credit card in the mail before their first official workday at the company.

"The core stuff that's the same across every role—assigning hardware, equipment, and getting to know people—is centralized with our operations team. The role-specific part of onboarding is left to the person running the department the new team member is joining." As a fully remote company it makes sense that the people in the support team follow an onboarding program relevant to them while developers follow a program that works for the dev team. Hotjar ensures that the different team leads speak to each other and share learning and best practices.

The company is divided into tribes, which are independent of teams. When someone joins Hotjar, they are automatically assigned a tribe based on their strengths and role. The tribes help ensure that individuals don't only interact with their functional teams. "We mix people up into different groups so that tribes have diversity. At the moment, when someone joins, they have to publish an article sharing 10 fun facts about themselves, which is a great way for people to get to know someone new."

4. BorrowMyDoggy

Rikke Rosenlund is the founder and CEO of BorrowMyDoggy, a company that aims to leave "pawprints of happiness on millions of dogs and people." According to Rosenlund, BorrowMyDoggy "is not just a company. It's a cause with a strong and authentic purpose. Every new employee must understand the depth of our purpose from day one of their onboarding."

In the early days of setting up the business, Rosenlund watched Simon Sinek's TED Talk[6] "How Great Leaders Inspire Action." As she explained to me, "The video focuses on asking 'why?' and it helped me to realize that this business is all about people and dogs making a positive impact on each other's lives, which was the same as my motivation for originally starting BorrowMyDoggy. We ask all new employees to watch the video to understand and relate to the company's purpose and why BorrowMyDoggy exists.

"We introduce the new employee to the various department heads and have a welcome lunch for them so they can introduce themselves and get to know the team better. A large part of our onboarding involves training, and we have all new employees, no matter what their seniority is, spend time dealing with customer services queries. The new employees will sit with the customer service team, learn from them, while spending time responding to customer queries." There is no better way to learn about a business quickly than to listen to its customers. Rosenlund uses this time to get new employees up to speed when it comes to developing an understanding of the customer. "We want them to feel firstly, like they have made the right decision to join us and secondly, that they can make a difference to our customers lives and the dogs they love, and the borrower's lives."

5. Jellyvision

Amanda Lannert, CEO of Jellyvision, has scaled the business from 40 when she joined to over 400 people and growing. The company develops software that "makes learning and decision-making delightful" by helping millions of employees understand their benefit options. The company, headquartered in Chicago, was founded in 2001 and has won numerous workplace awards, including 2019 *Inc.* Best Places to Work, 2018 *Entrepreneur* Best Company Culture, the *Chicago Tribune* Top Work Places 2015, 2016, and 2019, CityLight's Lighthouse Award Winner, and Moxie Awards.

Lannert described how the onboarding process has changed as the company has grown to hundreds of people. "As a company, we are continually evolving and improving, and our onboarding has probably changed more than in any department in the last year. For a company with 400 employees, the process during the first 90 days is incredibly curated." Lannert continued, "We have spent a ton of time learning how to create confidence and competence quickly. The process starts from the minute someone accepts the job offer. Once a candidate accepts to join, everyone they interviewed with sends them a welcome email. The moment of taking a job offer is a real moment of anxiety for people. It comes with butterflies and excitement and a bit of worry, so when the people who interviewed you tell you that they're so happy and can't wait for you to join, it is perfectly timed to help reduce the anxiety. It allows people to stand by their decision and feel good about it."

As the company has scaled, the team has had to adapt to hiring and onboarding large groups of new joiners at the same time. "One of our values, believe it or not, is *Embrace happy surprises; style points matter*. It sounds like a bizarre thing to have as a core value but it's indicative that we create experiences, not just for users but also for our customers, employees and people in the communities we are based in and part of." As a smaller company, they used to have new people stand up, introduce themselves, and have the whole company make a "stylish" orange juice toast. "However, as we scaled, we learned that it is tough to onboard 40 people in two weeks to do something like this organically. The 'happy surprise' tradition evolved: at the end of an employee's first day, and again at the end of their first week, when they get ready to leave the building, they get a standing ovation as they walk out of the building. It starts with their team and ripples out of the building as they go." Lannert explained the rationale behind the applause, "So why do we do it? At the end of your first day, you have come from the height of your power at your last job to the bottom of your power at Jellyvision. You're tired, anxious, emotionally exhausted, you probably need to pee, and you're completely confused. Through the ovation, we are saying, 'We get it. It will get better. Thank you so much,' but we do it in a surprising, and hopefully, lovely way."

6. Thread

Onboarding is a conversation at Thread; it's an ongoing back-and-forth process in which the company listens carefully to and observes the candidate and vice versa. As O'Neill explained, "Once an offer is accepted, we find out what equipment the candidates want, so that when they start everything is prepared from day one. We send a copy of the values document and the company handbook, so they've got that internalized before they start, too." Their hiring manager shares an "Excellence Document," which details what excellent performance looks like.

Delivering on Thread's *Commit to relentless self-iteration* value, there is a focus on employee development from the beginning of the Thread employment journey. Every new employee starts with a Development Plan based on feedback given during the interview process, so they have an improvement mindset baked into the new joiner from the outset. The Thread team takes the time to sit with new employees to share their feedback. O'Neill said that such feedback could be along the lines of: "When we were discussing hiring you, we felt that you were strong in these areas, which is why we hired you, and we thought that you could develop further in these other areas. What resonates with you, and which ones would you like to focus on as areas to develop and grow?" This system is an excellent way to demonstrate to new employees how essential feedback is in the company and how Thread cares about their growth and development.

7. Headliner

At Headliner, a platform that connects event planners directly to live musicians and DJs in the private events space, cofounder and CEO Stan McLeod believes in a culture of *transparency, freedom, self-expression* and *open communication*. He seizes the opportunity to showcase and improve this culture during every onboarding process.

McLeod and his team borrowed some inspiration from Mailchimp and Google regarding onboarding documentation. Headliner developed an onboarding document, and the responsibility for keeping it up to date is given to each new joiner after their onbaording. McLeod explained, "We ask them for their feedback about what worked and what didn't, and how we can improve onboarding. Then we ask them to update it. This way, the most recent new joiner is responsible for taking the version they received and improving it so that they can pass a better version on to the next hire."

8. Emarsys

Emarsys faces the challenge of having 16 offices around the world when it onboards new hires. CEO Ohad Hecht used to run the Asia region and back in the early days would have two full days of onboarding with every new employee. He was promoted to COO and moved to Europe, where he made a mistake of radically changing the onboarding process. "We would bring every new joiner to Vienna for two days of group onboarding, including 30 people, including the entire management team. This worked well initially, but I started to question whether getting everybody together for two days worked after a while." The issue for Hecht wasn't just that the senior management team was spending two precious days away from their day-to-day work—the main problem was that the company would see some new employees quitting their jobs soon after the induction. As Hecht explained, "Going to Vienna for some people was the main reason to come and have fun, and not everyone was that committed or came with the right intentions. They would enjoy the dinner, party, and get drunk and come in the following morning tired and not fully engaged. I found myself wondering why we were investing so many of our resources when it looked as if there was no ROI." Hecht eventually stopped the group onboarding process altogether. "About a year later I realized that I had made a mistake to stop the group onboarding. I realized that people remember the day they joined the company and many people are still very good friends with the people they met during those group onboarding days. People formed deep connections with colleagues from different offices, cultures, nationalities, and are still friends today. I decided to bring the group onboarding program back, with some changes."

The company now runs the group onboarding program every six weeks, and they switch the office where it is held, so for example in EMEA (Europe, Middle East and Africa) it rotates between London, Vienna, Berlin and Budapest. This allows new employees from other countries to meet, build friendships and absorb the local office culture. Local employees get to mix with the new people, giving them a chance to get to know them and share their local culture and knowledge of the business.

As Hecht said, "We have gone back to what worked in Vienna, but we have also improved on it by ensuring that the people we bring on are committed to joining the company and making a difference. We've developed videos about our culture, what's going on in the broader market and the local market conditions. We've also invested in training software that teaches the new joiners about our history, culture, who we are and what we stand for. Although we have added a lot of technology to onboarding, I still believe in personally being involved in the onboarding process, so anytime I can be there, I will."

9. SalesLoft

The SalesLoft recruitment process is longer than most. Once an applicant has accepted a position, there is an equally robust onboarding process, carefully designed to help people integrate into the business. In a world where far too many people still start a new job and find themselves twiddling their thumbs for the first few days or even weeks, SalesLoft ensures that their new joiners receive the necessary tools to succeed.

Each cohort of 10 to 12 new hires goes through two full days of onboarding orientation. Christine Kaszubski the Chief People Officer kicks off the two-day onboarding process with a video about the culture and then a talk. She acknowledges the intensive recruitment process and reiterates the values fit the new employees have with the company. "I explain that the core values probably show up in their personal lives; we've learned that they're inherently characteristics that our Lofters exhibit, and at SalesLoft we want everybody to bring their whole selves to work."

Kaszubski also explains that although they are new joiners, they are expected to become culture champions, "Not at 90-days, nor when they hit their first anniversary, but from their very first day onward. I encourage people to go talk to lots of people—outside their department, in the lunch line, wherever they can—to understand more about what the values mean to them." Those conversations help people understand how the values are applied and lived. "Because we don't have our values pasted on our walls. At SalesLoft it's all about how people experience and live the values and see others doing the same."

The new joiners then meet with leaders from every department, learn more about what sales enablement is and play with the platform. "We ask each new joiner, engineers included, to do a presentation describing and selling SalesLoft just like a salesperson would in an elevator pitch, which they then present on the second day." This is followed by developing a detailed 30-, 60-, 90-day plan that each person works through with their manager. The goal, Kaszubski explained, is "to ensure a fast start, which equals future success. The quicker people can feel connected, the more confident they'll feel in their role and the faster they'll integrate into the organization."

Interestingly, the company only has a probation period in the sales team, which has a boot camp that new salespeople have to complete successfully. "We don't get hiring right 100% of the time," Kaszubski explained, "so if somebody is not a fit with our values, we call it out early. But we don't have a specific probationary period." Kaszubski explained that she often hears from new Lofters that any early doubt about whether the culture is as good as the website says is surpassed by a feeling that it's even better than people thought. "Having that integration into the culture early on helps to solidify and verify that this is accurate, and this is how we work, and this is how we live."

For Kaszubski, being Chief People Officer is so much more than "just a job." "The other thing I try to instill in our new hires," she said, "is that when you are not happy at work, it affects so much of your life. Think about how many hours we spend at work. When you're not satisfied or not feeling valued, it affects your personal life, wellness, happiness and relationships. It is never lost on me that people choose to work at SalesLoft. I want to thank them for choosing us because they can work anywhere and we're in an exceptionally tight labor market." This drives Kaszubski to provide the best opportunities and environment for people to thrive. "I feel like I have the best job in the world because I have an opportunity to create better humans every day through the work we do."

When we spoke, Kaszubski had just launched a refreshed onboarding process and I asked her what the feedback had been, so far. "Although it's too early to tell, I've already seen the impact that it's had on new hires when they come back to me and say, 'On the outside of the company everybody's kind of like, is that company the real deal? And now that I'm here it's even better than I thought it was.'"

10. Next Jump

I first read about Deliberately Developmental Organizations (DDOs) in Robert Kegan and Lisa Laskow Lahey's book, *An Everyone Culture:*

Becoming a Deliberately Developmental Organization. DDOs are organizations that promote a culture in which employees can develop and pay attention to their personal growth as a part of their work environment. Kegan and Lahey's book opened my eyes to DDOs as the optimum of the company culture spectrum and an embodiment of the very future of work. They supply fascinating insights into what a DDO actually is and how it works. DDOs have a powerful mission to support humanity's innate desire to grow—and leverage that motive to ensure that both the organization and its people attain their full potential.

DDOs are ahead of their time because the work environment of a DDO cultivates authenticity and personal development. There is no lying, hiding or faking in a DDO. The individuals who work and thrive in a DDO environment allow themselves to be consumed by this one goal: to pursue their fullest potential, to excel in a daily competition against yesterday's self and then against all other competitors. They do this by believing in themselves and by studying and learning from their failures and faults. They are aware of both their strengths and weaknesses—and are constantly doing something about the latter.

Next Jump is one of only three companies Kegan and Lahey chose as examples of DDOs. I spoke with Becky Gooch, Head of Revenue, UK, and Graham Laming, a Software Engineer, to get a deeper understanding of the onboarding process that happens within their company.

Candidates who successfully pass the evaluations of Super Saturday—an event held three days a year, in which selected potential hires are flown in for a day of skills tests, exercises and interviews—receive an offer to join the company. They enroll in the Next Jump onboarding program: the Personal Leadership Bootcamp, or PLB. This period begins Next Jump's No Fire Policy. Perhaps it's a misleading title; most people would automatically assume that the employees abuse the situation given the knowledge that they can't be fired. Interestingly enough, that's not the case. This policy doesn't fully exempt anyone from being fired; if somebody breaks any of the fundamental rules (harassing someone, breaking the law, stealing from the company, etc.), they are naturally fired. Next Jump's No Fire

Policy means that an employee isn't fired for performance-related issues but is instead coached.

Here's why: the Next Jump team understands that the first months of an employee's experience at a company are the most crucial because these months heavily impact an employee's future with the business, how long they will remain with the company, their overall engagement and their long-term productivity. PLB is a significant upfront investment, since it is a program with no set length of time: you graduate to full employee status when you and your Talking Partner (more on that below) are ready. Some new employees take as little as three months to progress through PLB, others may take six or more.

Next Jump has developed an onboarding program of *doing* versus *showing*. They specifically work on emotional and character development by injecting stress early into the onboarding process. PLB is meant to be stimulating, engaging, fun, productive, challenging and deliberately stressful. This part of the program also comes with some distinctive elements:

- **A Closer Look at the Next Jump Story.** During PLB, new joiners learn of Next Jump's history and origins, its challenges and the lessons learned from obstacles and mistakes, and its vision as a company.
- **Skills Development.** New hires are expected to work on developing appropriate skills. For example, engineers can take different technical training courses and customer representatives undergo sales or marketing training; hires can begin the jobs that they were hired to do only after successfully graduating from the PLB program. Notably, new hires must also join the customer service team regardless of the role for which they've been hired. The company sets weekly (and steadily increasing) targets regarding the number of client tickets that a new hire is expected to solve and close.
- **Culture Development: Performance = Potential – Impediments.** Meanwhile, the company sets team challenges, surprise side projects, and other culture development initiatives that new joiners must complete and present to their team. Much of the program is

designed to help the new hires understand what personal behaviors or past experiences could hold them back from unleashing their full potential. Such initiatives allow these new hires to practice their fledgling skills and overcome their impediments in a "safe" environment where "failure" won't affect the business's revenues—thus the security implied from the No Fire Policy.

- **The Talking Partner.** During this program, candidates are individually paired with a Talking Partner (TP), who serves as a "deliberate release valve"; TP sessions are daily opportunities for candidates to chat about and share their issues, frustrations and thoughts about each coming day before beginning work. Ideally, these partnerships are formed between two individuals with opposite inclinations in terms of arrogance and insecurity; that is, one partner's personality leans slightly more toward confident/arrogant and the other partner's personality leans slightly more towards humble/insecure. Each TP partnership must graduate from PLB together.

- **The "Why" Statement.** The company pays for each new hire to attend Simon Sinek's online "Start With Why" course, enabling them to craft their own personal "why statement." This is meant to help newcomers realize not just their purpose, but also to take this understanding to another level and determine how their impediments might be getting in the way of them achieving that mission.

- **Continuous Feedback.** Feedback is paramount for growth and self-development, so the company presents each new hire with feedback made during the initial interviews and Super Saturday session. The hires see the thumbs up or thumbs down received on the recruitment app and are also provided with any additional comments (e.g., if they were perceived to be more confident/arrogant or humble/insecure). Feedback from the app is used as a starting point to develop each individual's self-awareness; the company develops this trait further through the candidate's situational workshops, peer feedback and the collaboration with their TP and coach. Over time, the new hires start to glean a better understanding of when and why their "backhand" (their weaker side—negative behaviors or tendencies) emerges in certain situations and how they can work on and improve it.

- **The Coach.** Each new hire is also paired with a coach: someone who is a relatively new hire and who has recently graduated from the onboarding process. During weekly or biweekly sessions, they discuss experiences regarding anything from the process of answering customer service tickets to involvement in culture initiatives. Coaches are meant to help the new hires probe into their struggles and the catalysts of these struggles, exploring the impediments to their potential success.

- **The Judges.** At the end of the first three weeks of PLB and every three weeks until graduation, the new hires must present to a panel of three judges and share these five things:
  - What they have been working on.
  - What they have learned.
  - The mistakes they have made.
  - The progress they believed they have made to strengthen their "backhand."
  - The work they have done to balance their arrogance or insecurity.

The judges then provide feedback; they must unanimously decide on a new hire's success before being officially inducted into the company. If a judge decides that someone is not ready to graduate, that new hire—*and* the partnering TP—must return to the PLB program and undergo three additional weeks of training.

The PLB program takes its members on a personal journey to understanding their strengths and weaknesses as well as their individual purpose in life. Just as importantly, it's about fostering within people the natural capability to *want* to develop themselves, so that when they graduate, they will not need to rely on PLB structures to continue their development. Each person's process is unique and cannot be compared to anyone else's; in most (if not all) cases, it's difficult to know if someone is ready to graduate and what "ready" really means to them. That's what makes PLB so unique, such a summary of many parts, and what makes it so valuable for each person.

PROBATION

Most new employees are on probationary status for a short period, generally 60-to 90-days. The employer must make sure that the person fits the values, can do the job and start to integrate them into the company culture. Or let them go if they're not a good fit. Like the onboarding process, many leaders treat probation as an afterthought and don't invest to ensure that the process is effective. This is an unusual approach if you consider that probation is the highest-value period for a company attempting to integrate the employee into the company. You have the fullest attention of the employee. They are still trying to find their feet and settle in, the least cultural bias (they're still new and not yet indoctrinated into the culture, so give you the most objective feedback), and the willingness to learn about and absorb the culture (right when they start).

There are several ways a company can use this time to ensure that the new hire is right for the company, and make sure that it is the right fit for the new hire.

This section explores companies that have designed effective probation candidate evaluation processes. Audiobooks has a three-month probation period that involves two anonymous surveys about the new employee to help the team's manager understand the rest of the team's feelings about the new person and gauge whether they fit with the values. Lillydoo has a six-month probation period in which a new hire and their manager have feedback sessions every two months, using a traffic light system of green, yellow and red to indicate if things are going well or not. And Aira has a set of expectation documents, which as the name suggests outlines precisely what the company expects from a new employee in their role.

1. Audiobooks

Sanjay Singhal is the founder of Audiobooks, a platform with over 150,000 audiobooks. Singhal, who also founded 500 Startups Canada, has developed a fascinating approach to ensuring that probation isn't just a rubber stamp affair.

To ensure that the wrong people don't join Audiobooks, they have a three-month probation period that involves two anonymous surveys about the new employee. The first survey takes place halfway through the probation period and the second happens just before the end of it. The former is a standard Net Promoter Score (NPS) survey asking everyone in the company who has interacted with the newcomer how they'd feel if they decided to leave and work for a competitor. Would they be upset, or would they shrug their shoulders and think "good riddance?" The NPS results inform the team's manager of the rest of the team's feelings and give senior management a sense of whether the newcomer fits into the culture. After the first survey, the manager meets with the new employee and discusses the NPS results.

Before the three-month probation period comes to an end, it's time for the second survey. The team who has worked with the new employee meets up and each person takes three cue cards, to score three questions on a scale of 1 to 10, with 1 being terrible and 10 being excellent. The questions are:

1. How would you feel if this person went to work for the competition?
2. How would you feel if you were stuck in an airport for five hours with this person?
3. How much would you trust this person to look after your child or pet?

Once everyone has marked their answers on the cue cards they are held up and shared with them. The results are discussed, and team members can be questioned and can explain their opinions. "No one can say that they weren't asked or that they didn't get a chance to have their say," Singhal pointed out. "It works really well—in some cases *too* well, from my point of view. I have had the group overrule me on candidates I liked and really wanted to hire. You can see the value of the process, as the team members—all of whom have progressed through the same probation period format—take this very seriously."

2. Lillydoo

Lillydoo has developed an employee probation process that allows the individual to know precisely where they stand regarding the progress they are making, or not, during their probation period. Cofounder & CEO Gerhard Kulack explained, "In Germany we have a six-month probation period and we have created a framework for the manager and the new employee to understand how the individual is progressing through the probation stage."

The company created a process during probation whereby the manager and the new employee have feedback sessions every two months. The aim of these sessions is for the manager to help the person get through the probation period. "The manager completes a one-page questionnaire about what the new joiner has been doing over the last two months detailing three things they've done well. The feedback includes a comment from the manager's manager and crucially, an opportunity area that the employee needs to work on during the next two months. The opportunity area is an area of their work where we think they should emphasize most on improving. It's not necessarily a weakness, but it could be. It could be about something that the person is good at and we believe that they should or could be doing better. Or it's just something they need to improve on."

To eliminate miscommunication, misinterpretation and make probation evaluation visible to everyone, the company created a green, yellow and red traffic light system. Green means things are going well and the new employee is on track; yellow means the person needs to improve in certain areas; and red is bad and the new employee is seriously off track. All new employees must be green to pass through the probation period.

"Just before the end of the six months, we ask the person's manager to reconfirm whether they would rehire them or not if they were to come in for an interview today. We ask them to think about the question, 'Would you hire this person today, considering the information you now have available to you?' The system works really well because it gives the employee a pretty good feeling of whether they are on track, and where to make improvements to get on track if they aren't. It also gives the manager a feedback framework with which to work during the probation period."

3. Aira

Paddy Moogan is the cofounder of Aira, a UK-based Digital Marketing Agency. Aira also has a six-month probation period with a similar yet different approach to evaluating a new employee's effectiveness in the role. "We are thorough with our time with probation because we really want to make sure the fit is right," Moogan explained. Each month, a new joiner will have a monthly check-in with their manager, followed by a quarterly review at the three-month mark, where they get structured feedback and, depending on the role, input from Moogan. "We will know in advance of their six-month probation whether they are struggling or not," he said, "because by that point they will have had concrete feedback on what's going well and what they need to do differently, and I'll have had a heads up from their manager if things don't feel right." Anything that hasn't been dealt with by the quarterly review is then followed up in months four and five. "The principle we try to work from is if they're not going to pass probation, it shouldn't be a surprise to anyone." Moogan explains that recently someone "beat us to the punch" before the six-month mark and voluntarily exited. "It was clear to everyone that it wasn't working and rather than dragging it out, we all agreed that it was best to call it a day at five months. An extended probation makes sense; after all, you're really just finding your feet for three months (the typical probation period in most companies). It's really between months three and six that you start to see if the person can do the job and the fit is right. Once people pass probation at six months, the full suite of benefits and perks kicks in."

Working with this level of rigor needs to be carefully thought through. I asked Moogan what a typical manager would review—is it their ability, or the fit with the company, or a bit of both? "A review starts with the concrete stuff around how someone is doing their job," Moogan explained. "We have a set of what we call expectation documents, which outline exactly what we expect from that person in their role. The starting point for the review is addressing whether they are hitting these areas." For example, a consultant is accountable for producing client-ready deliverables, defining client strategy and communicating well with clients to get work done. The document outlines, in detail, what excellent client deliverables are, what input into client strategy is required, how excellent communication builds trust and how the consultant needs to build up their commercial awareness and knowledge. "If there is a skills gap or another area that needs work it will be highlighted and will need to be worked on. The next layer of the review is to look at the culture and the fit. That part has been more about gut feeling until now because we've only just really defined our values." Moogan said, "What tends to happen is a subjective review of how that person is fitting in with the team and how well they're working with everyone. Are they trustworthy? Do people get on with them? That kind of thing. We've just finalized the definition of our values, so we're starting to implement our culture evaluation into the probation process. We will be asking the manager and the new joiner to discuss and evaluate how the new joiner is living the values during the probation period."

Moogan, who was running an office-based team prior to the pandemic, created with Aira's expectation documents an excellent example of how remote companies operate. By clearly setting out and communicating what Aira expects from a new joiner, the manager can monitor their progress, spot skills gaps or weaknesses and manage the individual accordingly without micromanagement. I will explore the importance of results- or output-based leadership for remote and hybrid companies later in this book.

PERFORMANCE EVALUATION

More and more companies are doing away with the traditional annual review process. It's an ineffective and inefficient process that looks back at an individual's performance, parts of which could have happened as long as 11 months ago. Instead, culture-driven companies implement an immediate feedback process and reward employees on a more regular basis for living the company's values. Some companies have replaced the annual review process altogether and others combine regular feedback with quarterly or biannual reviews.

Culture-driven companies view feedback as a muscle that can be developed and strengthened. It is an essential part of their operating system, one key driver of their companies' success, and they train their employees on how to give and receive feedback regularly and consistently. The companies I have interviewed use multiple types of feedback loops within their organizations, from performance reviews done by team members in which they set their own salaries, to monthly chats about how the person is living the values.

This section discusses how employees receive constant feedback at Jellyvision, where they have monthly written feedback between managers and employees. At CharlieHR, employees are assessed every month on how they lived the company's values. Performance evaluation is an ongoing exercise at Ballou, where they believe that no employee review should ever come as a surprise. Managers take monthly 20- to 30-minute walks with each member of their team at Runway to catch up and stretch their legs outside of the office and talk about work-related and personal challenges. Lillydoo proactively moves people through the promotion or salary increase process before employees ask for the raise or promotion.

1. Jellyvision

Amanda Lannert, CEO of Jellyvision, says that their strategy is to give constant feedback. "Everything we do in terms of feedback, surveys, pulses and performance reviews is about getting feedback in real time. If you do annual performance reviews, you do not get or give enough feedback. We do monthly written feedback between managers and employees in both directions: every employee does written feedback to their manager about how they think it's going against OKRs (Objectives and Key Results), and their manager feeds back to them. We invest in HR systems to make this as easy as possible, with things like trigger alerts, so that you can look and see the communication over time, the performance over time and what you said over time. It's an effective way to reflect quickly so that you can be more focused and successful moving forward.

"We focus on ways to have honest conversations around underperformance, and how to coach in those situations. When a company is small and there's underperformance, there's minimal coaching that happens. You part ways because you don't have time for underperforming people. As your business expands, you have a bit more leeway to make sure that people are coached and receive the feedback they need for their development."

2. CharlieHR

Founder and Chairman Rob O'Donovan explains that at CharlieHR employees are assessed monthly against the company's values. "We have one-to-one sessions where each team member meets with their team leader to discuss how they have embodied PACT (*Passion, Ambition, Curiosity, Together*) that month. It's not a typical review or appraisal session where we assess against targets or anything like that; it's more of an opportunity to sit down with the leader and discuss any range of things, including, but not limited to, areas where they're delivering on PACT or areas they need to work on."

On the one hand, the point is to remind the team that they all share the same values, that they should be proud of them, and that they must work hard to uphold them. On the other hand, O'Donovan knows that his people's work-life balance is exactly that: a balance. One arena can influence the other, e.g., a traumatic event in one's personal life will affect professional performance, however temporarily. Whenever necessary, team members must be heard and helped, as their health and lives are interconnected and can thus affect the business's health. "The open sessions are structured to be welcoming and personal, allowing team members to discuss anything that might be bothering or frustrating them in their professional and even personal lives."

3. Ballou

Performance evaluation is an ongoing exercise at Ballou, the award-winning Pan-European, integrated PR agency for high-growth technology companies. CEO Colette Ballou has a mantra that "no employee review should come as a surprise, ever." She explained that this is a mistake of traditional PR firms, as it indicates nothing but miscommunication or a lack of communication altogether. "If you are surprised by what you hear at your review it simply means that the manager has not communicated effectively to the employee prior to the review. At Ballou, we work on and agree on a plan with each member of the team; if you start to go off track, we discuss that and work on it with you as soon as we notice it. If there's negative or unsuitable behavior, the manager will have an offline conversation as soon as it is flagged. We try to understand the employee's side of the story, explain that they won't get ahead in the company behaving this way, and reiterate our values. If an employee's behavior needs to be corrected, we correct it immediately and always communicate with respect. We don't let it stagnate and we never call it out publicly. We know that employees are not deliberately trying to destroy the company and understand that they will make mistakes. By dealing with problems immediately in this way, there aren't surprises at the employee review stage."

4. Runway East

Natasha Guerra, CEO of Runway East, implemented a monthly GAD talk. GAD is short for *Give A Damn*, which is one of the company's four values, and the talk is an opportunity for the managers to spend 20 to 30 minutes meeting with each member of their team. Guerra explains that the GAD talks allow the management team to take some time out to catch up and keep up to date with how their team are doing. "This is an opportunity for team members to talk about what's on their mind. It shouldn't be work-related. It may be about how the person is doing, a personal challenge they may be facing, the upcoming weekend or any random questions they may want to ask." The company has developed a Personal Development Plan (PDP) for each employee and that is the only thing that is mandated to be discussed during each GAD talk. "We decided to include the PDP during the GAD talk because these catch ups are about how the team member is feeling or doing. It is a great time to understand how they are delivering against their Personal Development Plan and if there is any way that the manager can help."

5. Lillydoo

Lillydoo's CEO and cofounder Gerald Kullack meets with his leadership team every quarter to review how the employees in each team are doing, and when they received their last promotion or salary increase. If an employee is doing well and delivering in their role, the company will proactively move them through the promotion or salary increase without the employee asking. As Kullack said, "We believe that the happier a person is, the longer they will stay with us, the more they will learn and the better they will be at their job. We try to be a step ahead of the employee to surprise them with our recognition of the excellent work they are doing."

This quarterly review dovetails with an annual review Lillydoo has implemented, where they ask the employee to describe what goal they want to achieve at the company. "If we have a Supply Chain Manager and their goal is to become VP Supply Chain, we would not only give them regular feedback throughout the year on how we think they're doing their job, but also whether we think they are on track to reach their goal at Lillydoo." This review helps the company understand what the individual wants to achieve at the company. If the company doesn't believe the individual will be able to achieve that at Lillydoo they inform the person early on, which has the effect of managing expectations and taking the stress out of the situation.

According to Kullack, the company is growing so quickly that this situation has not happened very often. "We try to treat everybody in a very respectful way so that they have the sense that if I take care of my job, and take care of the business, the company will take care of me. This is undoubtedly one of the reasons why we haven't had anybody important leaving the company in the first four years of the business."

EXIT INTERVIEWS

If you have built a constructive, open, honest and trusting culture you should almost not need to conduct an exit interview. There are no surprises in trust-based cultures when a person decides to leave your company because they will have discussed their situation and reasoning with you during the many conversations, one-on-one meetings or feedback sessions that happened before their actual leave date. These conversations will often occur months before the person leaves the company, making a typical exit interview redundant. By the time they go, any feedback about their experience, the role or the company will have already been given and you will have made any necessary preparations required to fill the gap.

In high-trust, open and honest cultures an exit interview should be used to explore areas for company improvement, confirm and document the feedback you have already received, and ensure that the person will be a positive promoter of your business.

In cases where the culture is not as constructive, open, honest and trusting an exit interview can be an opportunity. You can find out why the person has decided to leave, what could have been done differently and anything that could be done to make them stay (if you want them to stay). Most people do not decide to leave a company on a whim and will have thought long and hard about their dissatisfaction, so it's crucial to know the real reason. People join companies, but they leave their managers, so you must try to understand any critical issues and determine how the company could improve and prevent this from happening with other employees.

Natasha Guerra, CEO of Runway East, said, "We find that our PDP (Personal Development Plan) process helps us understand where our team is regarding their career and longevity with the company. We use the PDP to understand what each individual wants to achieve in the next 12, 24, and 36-plus months. In some cases, we are not going to help them fulfill their longer-term goals at Runway East, but in the short- or medium-term, we can. Whether we can or not becomes apparent from the PDP process. Managers stay on top of their team member's progress toward their PDP goals through the monthly one-to-one GAD (*Give A Damn*) walks, and in the majority of cases it's not a surprise when an employee decides to leave the company."

IN CONCLUSION...

There is a tendency to believe that you can relax as your new hire has signed the contract to join. They're in. Done. But that could not be further from the truth. This is just the beginning of your journey together as colleagues. Like in the early days of a relationship, you get to know one another better, and you both regularly review their fit with your company. You have further opportunities to continue to assess your new hire (and for them to continue to assess you!) throughout onboarding, probation and performance evaluation. If done well, every one of these stages provides new insights into both of you and, should those insights not be positive anymore, also allow for a correction mechanism which is efficient and pain-free.

Onboarding is usually the new joiner's first meaningful experience with a company's culture. First impressions matter and if the onboarding experience is poor and ineffective, you are setting that person up for failure. Once they have been deemed in alignment with the company values during the recruitment process, new joiners have a right to be taught to live those values and need to have clear expectations set of what's required of them. Performance evaluations shouldn't be a once a year discussion; the culture-driven leader is being deliberate about feedback and focuses on encouraging it to happen regularly, often in real time. And when someone is leaving the company, hopefully you have created an open-communication environment in which you clearly understand why that person is leaving and what, if any, changes you will need to make going forward.

Some key takeaways from this chapter include:

- Send new joiners a welcome package in the mail with reading material, company branded clothing, and invite them to attend company events before they start work to make them feel like they're already a part of the team.
- Have everyone who interviewed the new hire send them a welcome email to alleviate any anxiety.
- Give them feedback that was gathered during their interview process and use that feedback as a personal development tool.
- Have every new joiner give their feedback on what worked in the onboarding process, what didn't, and how you can improve the process.
- Partner new joiners with a buddy from the team who makes sure that they get up to speed quickly, are integrating well, enjoy onboarding, and understand the company culture.
- Conduct values-based NPS (Net Promoter Score) surveys about the new joiners to understand better the rest of the team's feelings about the new person and gauge whether they are fitting into the culture.

- Evaluate new joiners as an ongoing exercise, so that no employee review ever comes as a surprise.
- Move people through the promotion or salary increase process without the employee asking.
- Actively try to help employees reach their career goals through coaching and feedback.
- Use the exit interview process as a chance for you to learn about the reasons an employee is leaving, if you don't already know, and to understand what you can do differently going forward.

Chapter 7

Bad Hires and Brilliant Jerks

"I'd rather have a hole in my organization than an asshole."
– Fred Wilson, Cofounder of Union Square Ventures

Hiring the wrong person can be a huge misstep and especially destructive during the early stages of a company's development. It can translate into a big setback or even catastrophic failure for the business. Many of you have probably been there done that: it can take a lot of management time and energy to undo the hiring decision and let go of the person who did not prove to be right for the job and/or for the team.

What is the difference between a bad hire and a brilliant jerk?

Bad hires happen because the person hired can't do the job, or because they won't do the job (they were misled about the role or misunderstood it during hiring) and because they do not fit the values of the company. Even someone who does the job okay but does not fit the values of the company is a bad hire. A bad hire will have a negative impact on the culture and the morale of the team, and will, at the very least, slow your business down; they can disturb the mood and mentality of your team, snuff out enthusiasm, and severely impact performance levels.

Brilliant jerks don't fit the values of the company either. But, unlike your classic bad hire, they are exceptionally good at their job. As their name suggests, brilliant jerks are often brilliant, charismatic and high-achieving individuals. They often come with a strong pedigree and deliver in the short-term, but at what long-term cost?

Together with their "brilliance," a brilliant jerk can be any, or all, of the following:

- Arrogant and headstrong.
- Inflexible, unable and/or unwilling to change.
- Create tension among team members, causing the need for unnecessary management intervention.
- Focused only on themselves and what they want to achieve.
- A manipulative figure in the team.
- Lacking in personal accountability.
- Inspire imitation, thereby exacerbating the problem across the company.
- Create a culture of dependence.
- Bring doubt within the team regarding the leadership's commitment to the company's values, and specifically their commitment to hiring the right people.

Whether they're brilliant jerks or simply bad hires, employees who are not a good fit with the values of the company should be terminated as quickly as possible.

Brilliant jerks can be particularly difficult to fire. How can you fire someone who looks to be performing so well? A fast termination is both in the employer's and the employee's best interest: there are companies that are better suited for the way the brilliant jerk works. You are doing them, your company and your team, a disservice by keeping them on your payroll. Letting them go fast doesn't mean you have to abandon them or treat them badly. You may not be able to afford to help them financially with a generous severance package like Hotjar does, but it makes sense for your HR and recruiting team to offer help in finding them their next job.

Weeding out a brilliant yet toxic employee quickly, is paramount to preserving the long-term culture and health of your company.

It should be noted here that understanding your culture and what drives the business is vital. If your culture revolves (and is designed) around individual contribution and the brilliant jerk fits the values of your business, then there is no reason why they shouldn't thrive. But if collaboration and teamwork are critical ingredients for your organization's success, then weeding out a brilliant yet toxic employee quickly is paramount to preserving the long-term culture and health of your company.

The issue lies in the fact that the CEO is often unaware of the jerk's behavior, or turns a blind eye to it, and doesn't realize the negative effect the jerk is having on the rest of the team until it's too late. Imagine the scenario where a first-time founder and CEO is encouraged by their investors to hire one of the most brilliant, visionary people. The founder expects great things because this person is a genius and they work well together on a one-to-one basis. The new employee has taken on a lot of responsibility, freeing up the founder to focus on the strategy of the business. From the founder's perspective it all seems rosy, but what the founder doesn't realize is that the new hire is dictatorial with peers and junior members of staff, dominates the conversation in meetings, doesn't listen to anyone else on the team, won't share information, and is abrasive and rude toward members of the opposite sex. The founder wouldn't know that team morale is falling off a cliff. Yes, the jerk is brilliant, but to the rest of the team it is patently clear that their behavior is unacceptable and they don't fit in the company.

In this chapter I look at seven companies that make values fit a clear priority over skills and pedigree. The culture-driven leaders I interviewed have developed processes to ensure that they don't hire the wrong sort of person for their company, or that they reverse hiring mistakes quickly. Next Jump focuses on hiring people who demonstrate that they are coachable, hence willing and able to change and grow. Hotjar will eliminate a candidate from the process if something seems off, no matter how brilliant they are at their job. At busuu, it doesn't matter which company the candidate comes from, or what technical skills they have, if they don't fit the values they won't be hired. HubbleHQ leadership discovered that the pinch they may feel from firing a bad apple without an immediate replacement is worth it in the long run. At Audiobooks and Thread, leadership acts quickly to get rid of any bad apples that might have slipped through the net. Firing an employee who doesn't share the company's values triggers reflection and a values re-evaluation at Influitive.

1. Next Jump

I spoke with two Next Jump employees to get a deeper understanding of how the company avoids hiring brilliant jerks. Becky Gooch is Head of Revenue, UK, and Graham Laming is a Software Engineer. Both joined the company immediately upon graduating college and have been recipients of the rapid development that happens to employees at a DDO (Deliberately Developmental Organization) like Next Jump.

One of the many strengths and refreshing qualities of the Next Jump culture is that, as a business and as individual people, they are open about their failures and about learning from those failures. This includes their recruitment experiences of hiring brilliant jerks. In the early days, the company policy was to hire "the best" graduates from the top engineering and computer science schools, including MIT, Carnegie Mellon, Cornell, Columbia and Georgia Tech. The team hired those "top graduates" who were indeed stunningly brilliant people and driven to succeed. Yet, quite soon after onboarding, the Next Jump team discovered that they had in fact hired a bunch of "brilliant jerks," who were not team players and turned out to be very toxic for the culture.

The new hires lacked all traces of humility, couldn't deal with critical feedback, weren't prepared to fail, and were stubborn in the way that they approached their work. Realizing their mistake, Next Jump fired these brilliant jerks. As Gooch explained, "The team reviewed the experience and adapted the recruitment process to be more effective at finding the people we want to hire."

The company has designed a recruitment process around a one-day event called Super Saturday where they invite shortlisted candidates to come in for a day of interviews. The day is structured to evaluate the candidates for:
1. Ability to do the job.
2. A student mindset – are they humble, grateful and responsible?
3. Coachability – are they able to take and act upon the feedback they get during the team-based interactive elements of the interview?
4. Grit – do they have the resilience and self-confidence that people get from pushing through difficult and challenging situations before emerging wiser?

5. An understanding of their own strengths and weaknesses.
6. GAS – do they Give A Shit?

Lamming added, "We still hire from top schools, but one of the criteria we are evaluating against is whether or not a candidate is coachable—which brilliant jerks are not—and demonstrates the qualities that the company believes make the ideal Next Jumper."

2. Hotjar

David Darmanin founded Hotjar together with three friends who all live on the island of Malta. "In the beginning there were four of us—three Maltese and one Swede—all living just a few kilometers away from each other. Yet we treated each other and worked as if we were remote workers in the same team. It was a counterintuitive move. We avoided face-to-face meetings, even social gatherings, we avoided making decisions in person and I insisted that we should not start working together in person too much. It was a very successful move because when more people joined us remotely later on, they fit in automatically and didn't feel left out." Being able to hire remote employees was practically essential for the company; being on a tiny island in the middle of the Mediterranean didn't provide great quality or diversity when it came to the talent pool.

Perhaps the most critical of the remote work challenges is the risk of under- or overestimating people due to the physical distance between individuals and the lack of face-to-face interaction. With remote working, Darmanin explained, it's much easier to overestimate or underestimate people and situations because "there's more of a gap and your mind can easily fill in the blanks." If a team isn't careful or thorough enough when hiring, things can get messy. "You think: 'Well, there was a misunderstanding' or 'Things will get better,' but because you're not there face-to-face to see how someone is working, it's easy to make assumptions. We learned that you really need to hire painfully slow and fire very fast in order to ensure that there are no doubts and that it's the right fit."

In growing Hotjar, Darmanin has seen his share of brilliant jerks. He recalls a time when the company interviewed a very strong developer (an ex-Googler) who aced the code tests. "We asked him to tell us about a time when he had a conflict at work. He told us about a scenario where he worked on a team with just one female colleague. He'd said, 'Oh, we should tell what's-her-name, the girl, the girl on the team' and his manager overheard it and asked the developer to use her name as much as possible, citing that 'She might not like it and it can come across as insensitive.' The developer explains that he got really annoyed that he was corrected about this, and he said something like, 'It makes no sense. If she's a girl, she's a girl.' The fact that he didn't even understand why this was a concern for his manager, for us, was such an easy red flag and irrespective of how brilliant he was or where he came from, we weren't going to hire him."

3. busuu

Bernhard Niesner, cofounder and CEO of busuu, explained that his team has created a series of interview questions that the company uses to evaluate whether or not a candidate fits with the values of the company. "If there is no fit with our values, we won't hire a candidate—it doesn't matter if they're the best engineer from Google or Facebook; if they don't match the values, they won't be hired. These values have helped us build a great team over the last couple of years. Another positive of having our values clearly defined is, if we do make a hiring mistake, it's extremely obvious; we see it quickly and take action immediately. In the one or two cases where we have made a mistake, the newcomer often realized the mismatch before we did and left the company of their own accord."

It is unrealistic to expect to not make any hiring mistakes; and, in fact, recognizing the mistakes and dealing with them quickly is the important bit. Some leaders—knowing in their gut that the newcomer isn't the right fit—make the mistake of "gifting" that person an extended chance to see if they might hopefully and eventually manage to mesh with the rest of the team. A lot of leaders fall into this trap. This doesn't just contribute to further delays and doubts, because you're postponing the inevitable; it can confuse and upset the team. Your employees are watching closely to see who you hire into the team and they watch even closer when you *don't* fire someone who is clearly a wrong values match. They don't want to work with a jerk. They want the reassurance—each time—that you'll continue to hire people with the right attitude, who can do what's expected of them, are cooperative and trustworthy and whose values match the team's.

Niesner understood this quickly: "In the past, we'd give a questionable candidate some time because they were trying hard. But now we are clearer on what behaviors and outcomes we expect from our people, so it is now really obvious from early on that they don't fit. We don't waste the person's time in a company that's not right for them and we don't want to waste our time with the wrong person. Things are done a certain way at busuu. If a person doesn't fit our culture, it is better that they work in another environment where they do fit."

4. HubbleHQ

HubbleHQ's cofounders Tushar Agarwal and Tom Watson understand that firing an employee who is not a good fit quickly is a key element that contributes to building the right team. Agarwal and Watson said, "Looking back now, we realize just how helpful and valuable it was for our approach to hiring and firing, to have invested the time in defining our company's mission, vision and values when we did early on."

They described one unsuccessful hire they made and the valuable lesson they learned from the experience. "It was our mistake since it was early on in our development as a company and we didn't qualify the candidate against our values thoroughly enough. One of our company values is empathy and although it didn't come across in the interview the new hire turned out to be inconsiderate and insensitive. It was clear after just a couple of weeks that the person didn't embody the culture of the company." When Agarwal and Watson fired the bad apple, they realized that having him gone was a great relief. While a few members of the team needed to step in and fill the role for a brief period of time, most importantly the air cleared and the increasingly negative feeling in the team was replaced with a strength of conviction and reassurance of having done the right thing.

5. Audiobooks

According to Sanjay Singhal, Canadian tech entrepreneur and cofounder and former CEO of Audiobooks, "Everything begins with trust. An absence of trust results in the team members being unable to show their weaknesses; to be vulnerable and open with one another.

The absence of trust is a huge waste of time and energy because team members waste this time and energy in defensive behaviors instead and are reluctant to ask for help from—or assist—each other. I have found that teams can overcome this dysfunction by sharing experiences, demonstrating credibility and developing strong insight into the unique characteristics of other team members."

Singhal is adamant about firing fast when it comes to bad hires or brilliant jerks. He prides his business for having high standards and reports no qualms for firing folks who don't live up to those standards or the business's core values. Singhal explained, "If you don't act quickly, any negativity or cultural mismatch will spread across the company like cancer and destroy the good work that you've done over the years in building it. This high standard goes for everyone in the company. Our executives are subject to anonymous employee reviews, and I will fire an executive immediately if two or more people agree that there has been a serious lack of living up to the company values."

6. Influitive

Influitive's Executive Chairman Mark Organ discussed how he uses senior executive terminations to re-evaluate the company values. Analyzing why a senior executive hire didn't work allows the company to review the values and the interview process to see where the system failed. Organ said that he agonizes over two processes in his business: promotions and firings. "The only thing worse than keeping an employee who doesn't live the values, is promoting someone who isn't living the values." Organ makes a very good point. Promoting an employee who doesn't live the values only rubs salt deeper into the wound for the people who have to work directly with them. "Our experiences have demonstrated that it doesn't matter if you are successful at delivering the product or closing the big deal; if you don't live the values, you will not progress and you will be let go."

Organ experienced the pain of unexpected culture clashes during the early days of Influitive. He and his cofounder couldn't agree on the direction of the business, and it turned out that they had fundamentally different leadership styles. Organ was in the fortunate position where he could buy out the other cofounder. "This triggered some naval gazing, because I realized that something in the original values we created had clearly not been communicated properly, or was left unsaid between us. Our small team had a rethink, eliminated some values, added others, and every high-profile executive that we have lost since then—whether through resignation or firing—has triggered a review of our values." When we spoke, Organ explained that he had recently fired an executive who struggled to engage with the team, even though they were an incredibly skilled person. This resulted in another values review where the team had the realization, based largely on the fired employee's behavior, that there was vital value missing: "At the time," Organ said, "we didn't have an explicit value about *team empowerment*; that's when we decided that it was a value that we had to add to the list."

7. Thread

Thread CEO Kieran O'Neill has also let people go when they didn't match company values, despite the fact that many of them were excellent performers otherwise. According to O'Neill, enforcing the right culture in your business begins with leading by example. "For me, the biggest test of how much you live your values is whether you reject someone who is awesome at his job's functional skills but has a big question mark over their ability to live the values. It's easy to let go of somebody who is bad at both. But it's hard to say, 'Hey, Mr. Engineer, you are incredibly brilliant and productive, but I am sorry— you don't match our values.' That has happened at Thread."

O'Neill reiterated that policing the culture is never a one-man job. His team has sounded the alarm and instigated the removal of a bad apple, just as O'Neill has himself. "It's not just about me as CEO being the 'values guy,' it's everybody's responsibility."

IN CONCLUSION...

Everybody makes hiring mistakes and bad hires or brilliant jerks could slip through the net. If you start to evaluate candidates through the lens of your company's culture, specifically your values and expected behaviors, it becomes easier to spot them, avoid them or—if you've already hired them—let them go quickly. The benefit to your business in the long-term, of letting them go, outweighs the short-term challenges of covering that position until it is filled again.

To avoid hiring bad hires and brilliant jerks:

- Develop a robust recruitment process that includes values-based interview questions.
- Evaluate for brilliant jerk tendencies by testing their ability and willingness to accept feedback, to change and grow.
- Involve your employees more in the hiring process and make it everyone's responsibility to spot problem candidates.
- Empower your employees to speak up and call you on it anytime they feel that a candidate could be a bad hire or a brilliant jerk.
- Do not hesitate to continually re-evaluate, tweak and adapt your values or process to reflect learnings from situations when the system fails.
- Fire quickly and respectfully if a bad hire or brilliant jerk has slipped through the net.

Chapter 8

How to Embed Company Culture

"Every CEO is in fact a Chief Cultural Officer. The terrifying thing is that it's the CEO's actual behavior, not their speeches or the list of values they have put up on posters, that defines what the culture is."
– Scott Berkun, Author, *Making Things Happen: Mastering Project Management*

Embedding a company culture—so that what you say is what you do—while straightforward if you understand the fundamentals, is a familiar blind spot for many CEOs. A failure to embed culture properly is a primary contributing reason for many companies' inability to operate over the long-term as high-performing businesses.

Picture the CEO of a 20-person startup who keeps telling their team that customer service is a top priority. One of the company's values is *We WOW our customers*, but the CEO doesn't invest in the software that the customer service manager says is required to offer a "wow" level of service. Do you think they mean what they say? Or what if they don't measure any of the critical metrics on customer service? What if they fail to encourage their customer service team to learn and develop new skills, and never offer them opportunities to improve themselves? What if they never reward or recognize the hard work accomplished by the customer service team? What if they leave the team understaffed? Do you think this leader is genuinely interested in customer service? Do you think their team believes them when they claim that they are? Is there any consistency between their words and their actions?

Sadly, no. They don't practice what they preach. The customer service team is aware of it, and so is the rest of the company. The team collectively rolls their eyes every time the leader mentions the "importance" of customer service. The inconsistency starts to breed distrust and doubt about the other claims the leader is making, leading to culture degradation and dysfunction.

Paying lip service to espoused values is among the most self-sabotaging ways to undermine a culture.

CEOs like this may want their company to *WOW their customers*, but they either don't focus on living the values, or neglect them altogether. They tend to believe that since they have written a list of values and had them printed on posters and coffee cups, their teams will somehow live up to those values instinctively. Paying lip service to espoused values is among the most self-sabotaging ways to undermine a culture. Saying one thing and doing another sows doubt among the team about the company's real values. Eventually, this destabilizes the team and negatively impacts motivation, engagement, commitment, productivity and loyalty.

To get a better understanding of how to embed culture, we look at the work of MIT Professor of Management Edgar H. Stein in his ground-breaking book *Organizational Culture and Leadership*. Schein—the godfather of company culture—talks about the six primary embedding mechanisms:

 I. How and what you reward and recognize.
 II. How you hire, promote and fire.
 III. What you consistently measure or pay attention to.
 IV. How you guide the team in investing or allocating funds in the business.
 V. How you coach, teach, and educate.
 VI. How you react to failure, emergencies, critical issues, and other company crises.

These mechanisms are self-explanatory and describe what happens daily in a company. Do you hire or promote the right people in line with your company values? Do you really prioritize the things that you say are important? What else, apart from the numbers, do you measure in the business? Where in the company do you allocate funds? How do you encourage employees' personal development? And the most difficult one perhaps—because you may not have time to think before reacting—how do you behave in the heat of an unexpected product failure?

In this chapter I review each embedding mechanism and explore how different companies utilize them to strengthen their culture.

I. WHAT YOU RECOGNIZE AND REWARD

You can demonstrate to your team what you, as a leader, most value through the way you recognize, reward or penalize your people. Some companies are deliberate about giving both recognition and rewards; others only give recognition. Consider the difference between rewarding and recognizing and then decide what's right for your business:

- Rewards are consumed and transferable, whereas recognition is experienced by the receiver.
- Rewards are transactional and recognition is relational.
- Rewards are outcome-driven and expected.
- Recognition is often a surprise.

They are also linked:

- Rewards are tangible and have a specific value and you should always give recognition when you give a reward.
- Recognition is intangible and you can give recognition without reward.

The nature of the behavior rewarded or penalized, and the kind of rewards or penalties themselves, will embed (i.e., more deeply ingrain) what you value and prioritize.

One way to ensure that the company's values are understood and adopted is by creating reward and recognition initiatives around them. Doing this requires you to define the expected behaviors related to those values and then link the reward and recognition with those behaviors.

This section discusses Pardot's monthly "Hero" and "Hassle" awards and how Unbounce gamifies the recognition element of its culture.

1. Pardot

David Cummings, founder of Atlanta Tech Village, described how his former company Pardot, which he founded and led, focused more on recognizing the living of the values rather than the business numbers. "As a company, we had our goals and our quarterly OKRs (Objectives and Key Results), but from a recognition point of view, we focused almost exclusively on the culture side of things."

The company had two categories of awards every month, one dedicated to the "Hero" and one dedicated to the "Hassle." The Hero of the Month award was for the person who demonstrated the living of the values. The Hassle of the Month award was for the person who suggested the best idea to solve a company problem or issue.

For the Hassle of the Month, the company set up an idea exchange, which was like a message board, where people could add ideas and then vote the ideas up or down. As Cummings explained, "A hassle could be anything in the business that was slowing an employee down or stopping them from doing a better job—something that literally was a hassle! It could be a software issue, a people issue, an infrastructure issue—such as how long it took to get certain answers for our customers, or there being too few healthy snacks in the break room—whatever people felt was slowing them down from being the best they could be and doing the best work they could do." To make it a democratic process, everybody got one vote per month per category.

The Hero and the Hassle would be recognized at the monthly All Hands meeting. The Hero's nominator would stand up and share why they had nominated the Hero, and the Hero would receive a $100 prize. For the Hassle, the person who submitted the chosen hassle would say why they submitted that idea, suggesting their thoughts on fixing it; they too would receive $100. The winners would also receive a garden gnome, which they could display on their desk for the following month.

Cummings added, "We focused on developing a culture of continuous improvement where we were always trying to get better at everything we did. These rewards worked extremely well for us."

2. Unbounce

Unbounce CEO Rick Perreault gamified his company's values with the creation of "core value cards." Perreault explained that, "If someone notices a fellow employee living a value, then they are encouraged to write it down on the relevant core value card and share it with that person. This has turned out to be a very successful tool because our people are now collecting the core value cards and you can see them piling up on people's desks. Noticing one of the values—like a courageous act—and writing the act down on the card, and then giving the card to the person, is a great way to remind people that these values are really important." Gamification has added a fun, visual element to the recognition of the values and as Perreault admitted, "Work can get tough at times and it's a really nice surprise when, out of the blue, someone notices what you've done and thanks you for it."

II. HOW YOU HIRE, PROMOTE AND FIRE

How you select and hire new team members provides a powerful insight into whether you, as the leader, are living the values. Your team is expecting you to hire someone who fits the values. Your team will assess each new hire and will rapidly discover whether you've hired someone who aligns with the company's values or not.

The way people interpret the decision-making criteria around internal promotions can encourage specific behaviors that work for or against your culture. Promoting someone for the wrong reasons, or someone the team believes does not truly live the values, will be detrimental to the culture you are building. Similarly, how you fire someone and the perceived or understood reasons for their firing can impact your culture. Firing the brilliant jerk who was not a good fit with your values will strengthen it.

Keeping the values at the forefront as you decide who to hire, promote or fire is crucial. There should be no doubt that the person you are hiring or promoting can live the values. If you employ someone who isn't a good fit with the values, there should also be no doubt that they will be terminated. It is easier, both emotionally and practically, to bring yourself to deal with it quickly.

This section discusses how the Hotjar founders learned early on that if you hire someone who doesn't fit the culture, you need to let them go quickly and with respect. I also look at SalesLoft's in-depth, resource-intensive and time-consuming recruitment process.

1. Hotjar

"After our first hire, we managed to get hiring completely wrong!" CEO David Darmanin stated about what they learned at Hotjar in the early days of the company. Darmanin told me that, in the beginning especially, the company hired the wrong people. They had to let go of one person quickly, within days of the person joining the company. "There were clear indicators that the person wasn't right for the culture and the team. They had an attitude problem and didn't communicate well, so we knew instantly it was a poor fit."

Hotjar demonstrates a commitment to the value, *building trust with transparency* by not tolerating employees who have the wrong attitude—terminating that employee communicated the unacceptable nature of that type of behavior or attitude. As a leader, you must remember that your team bought into the culture and values you described when they joined your company. They expect you to continue to recruit people who fit the values. They will also understand that mistakes happen, that the wrong person may slip through the net and get hired. They will trust and respect you more if you act quickly when you realize it.

Hotjar also found that even though it might seem financially inconvenient, it's good to give the person leaving one-, two- or three-months' pay to lessen the blow and ease any ill will toward the company that the person may have. "The reality is with remote work, you risk pulling out the cords from someone connected to you virtually, which means that suddenly, they might be out there alone. Because you don't have the chance to say goodbye in person, it helps to soften the landing." Hotjar demonstrates the value *Work with respect* by giving a generous termination payment, showing that they care for their employees, even if they don't work out for the company.

2. SalesLoft

SalesLoft spends a lot of time making sure that the people they bring into the company can do the job and match the business's values. The SalesLoft hiring process includes a recruiter screen, manager screen, peer interview, a TopGrading interview, an interview with the Chief People Officer and a core-values interview. VP-level candidates will also meet with three of the four-person executive leadership team. Christine Kaszubski, Chief People Officer, said, "Although our hiring process is longer than most, we've been able to prove that our process works and is scalable. We have experienced 250% employee growth over the past 24 months. When I joined the company at the end of 2017, we were 170 people and are now over 450 and, not only have we sustained our culture, but we've continued to strengthen it."

Kaszubski continued, "Our Lofters understand that they have a voice in everything we do, especially in how we select individuals that join SalesLoft. This is where the core-values interview team comes in." The core-values team consists of people who were voted for by their manager to join the team. Kaszubski personally interviews them to assess their suitability for the role and once selected, they go through training to ensure that they can evaluate a candidate's fit with values. Two employees (a male and a female) always conduct the core-values interview. The extended interview process works. "New employees report feeling a strong sense of connection with the company from day one. We also have a significantly lower than industry average turnover rate of 18% versus 30% and our people stay with us for longer."

During our conversation, Kaszubski was very clear on one factor of company culture that many leaders don't grasp: "Our company is not for everyone. If a candidate doesn't fit the values, it doesn't mean that there's anything wrong with them. It just means that they're not a fit for the SalesLoft." Kaszubski emphasized that they want every person who goes through the hiring process to have gained more clarity on who they are and which values matter most to them. "The process makes candidates think about the type of company that they should be looking to join. If a candidate gets two offers and they are a better fit in the other organization, I'd rather them take that offer because it's better for them and better for us. If our recruitment process helps that, then everyone wins."

III. WHAT YOU MEASURE OR PAY ATTENTION TO

Your company's areas that receive systematic attention over the longer term—the things you spend time monitoring—reflect what you prioritize and ultimately what's going to be embedded into your culture. What you systematically remark on, comment about or notice, measure, or pay attention to, will send clear signals to your team about your values and what's important to you. If you measure something, it's important to you, and the team will respond to that measurement by trying to deliver the right outcomes. If you don't measure something, it is not as important as the things you do measure.

Being deliberate about what you give importance to becomes a powerful way of communicating the culture you want to build. If you pay attention to too many things or are inconsistent in what you pay attention to, your team will use their judgment to decide what's essential, resulting in a dysfunctional culture.

This section explores how Periscope uses employee engagement surveys to uncover potential issues and how Influitive incorporates three out of the six primary embedding mechanisms into a daily nine-minute all-hands meeting.

1. Periscope Data

Melanie Tantingco, Regional VP People Operations at Periscope Data, runs an employee engagement survey every six months. "Pulsing our employees allows me to identify the blind spots specifically. We don't alter the survey questions, so we get to see a six-month comparison." When Tantingco and her team look at the results, they rank the issues and decide what actions need to be taken over the following six months. "Some of the most eye-opening slices of the data are when we do one-on-one meetings with each manager. We go through the results of the survey with them to say something along the lines of, for example, 'When you look at your heat map, it looks like the males on your team feel like they have more work-life balance than the females on your team. The difference is significant. Do you know why that might be? Could this be tied back to a comment that you've made, or something like that?' Digging into the data helps to make the managers hyper-aware of their influence."

Tantingco presents the results of her surveys to the board of directors, focusing on three different outcomes. "One: are we a better employer than all the other companies that use the same survey tool, especially tech companies of a similar size? Two: what do the comments tell us we are doing really well, and what are our opportunities to improve? And three: when I start slicing and dicing the data based on different demographics, are we unfairly treating any demographic?" Tantingco looks to see if anything statistically significant stands out in the survey results, like with males versus females, parents versus non-parents, or managers versus individual contributors versus executives.

By digging into the pulse survey data at this level of detail during a manager's one-on-one and the board meetings, Tantingco is embedding the values of *Inclusion*, being *Data Driven*, and *Transparency* across all levels of the company.

2. Influitive

At Influitive, Mark Organ and his team created a multi-layered value recognition system with daily, monthly, quarterly and annual events that promote the culture. "We have an all-hands meeting every day to get our team of 150 people together to share information about the company and recognize someone for living one of the values. We also recognize a 'hero of the quarter,' which is voted on by peers for attainment in company values and execution, and we have annual recognition awards for each of our values, which we celebrate at our holiday party."

A quirk of the Influitive culture is the company's daily global all-hands meeting, which runs for exactly nine minutes, from 11:51 to 12:00 Eastern Time. "At 11:47, we have music that plays in the office to let everyone know that they have to come to the boardroom." The nine-minute Daily Sync-Up meeting is mandatory for employees but is also open to anyone else who wants to attend. Organ explained, "We encourage employees to bring in potential candidates, friends, and family members to the all-hands meeting to involve more people and export our culture. This daily all-hands meeting is the business's heartbeat, and we use the same structure every day." The meeting minutes are written up and shared with the company, the board and the shareholders.

The nine minutes cover the following items:

- Introduce any new hires.
- Review yesterday's key metrics.
- Recognize qualified customer meetings, sales demos, customer wins and customer renewals.
- Have a three-minute departmental "deep dive" on what is currently happening in a department (this is the only element of the Daily Sync-Up that changes day-to-day; the department representative has three minutes to discuss insights, current events and lessons learned). Each department preps for its three-minute spotlight session; excellent communication, great content and the best presentation wins the monthly Department Spotlight Award.
- Discuss any good news either on a personal or professional basis.
- Recognize a team member for their daily embodiment of one of the company values.

The success of these daily nine-minute meetings isn't coincidental. There is a team member who is responsible for organizing the meeting and ensuring its seamless progress. "We invest a lot of time and effort in these meetings; therefore, we must get them right. We have a committee responsible for the health of the Daily Sync-Up meeting; they make sure that it's working well, collect feedback about the meetings and suggest changes as the result of the company feedback." Organ also said that this process didn't come to be overnight. "It's taken us years to get the daily all-hands meeting right." Influitive's nine-minute meeting uses three embedding mechanisms:

- Recognizing and rewarding individuals for living the values.

- Highlighting to the team the new hires that have been made.
- Measuring and paying attention to key metrics.

Bringing everybody in the company together, even sometimes their friends and family members, for this daily all-hands meeting does an exceptional job of spreading the culture and embedding Influitive's *Win as a team* value.

IV. HOW YOU INVEST OR ALLOCATE FUNDS IN THE BUSINESS

Where you choose to invest and where you don't, demonstrate what's critical to you and the business. The way budgets are created and how goals are set will reflect your beliefs about the company's priorities and its risk appetite.

Remember back to the CEO at the beginning of this chapter, who claimed that customer service was a priority, with the *WOW our customers* company value? The CEO would have demonstrated that customer service was indeed a priority for the business if they had allocated budget to buy the software requested by the customer services manager.

This section discusses the impressive and well-thought-through perks offered at Hotjar, how Unbounce offers cash to help make its employees' vacations more enjoyable, and how The Social Element uses a psychometric tool to categorize employees' behavior differences.

1. Hotjar

Fully remote company Hotjar invites the entire team to two retreats every year, paid for by the company, and gives each team member an annual allowance of $2,200 to encourage teams to meet up in smaller groups and work together. As CEO David Darmanin explained to me, "We know how much worth comes from getting to know each other in person. Our teams meet up several times a year for this reason, be

People Officer, Wendy, had a throwaway comment in a meeting a while back where she said, 'Well, remember, I'm an S. I'm not going to decide on this right now. I need to go away and have 24 hours to think about it.' Everyone in the meeting knew that she was referring to the fact that she doesn't like to be rushed to decide. Before we implemented DISC, she would not have felt confident in saying, 'I need a bit of time to think about this.' We can make use of our profiles to say, 'This is me. This is who I am, and hence I need to do this in this way,' and people can playfully make fun of each other and say, 'You're being a bit D there!'" Investing in training her entire team in understanding the DISC profiling technique has allowed the team to be more accepting and joke about each other's natures, while also getting a sense of people's default personality position. *Be one team* is one of the core values of The Social Element and investing in the DISC methodology has demonstrated how vital teamwork is. Littleton said that the DISC methodology has reinforced a core value and has provided a great benefit to the company. "It's given the team a valuable shared frame of reference for communication and to be more understanding of each other. Communication has improved and some of the internal tensions have definitely eased over time using DISC methodology."

V. PEOPLE DEVELOPMENT, COACHING, TEACHING AND ROLE MODELING

You need to be a role model, teacher and coach for the culture you want to build. To embed a culture, the leaders need to demonstrate living the values and spend time teaching and coaching their people to do the same. By learning how to handle customer service queries, and encouraging their team to do the same, leaders demonstrate how vital customer service is for their company.

When it comes to formal learning and development (L&D), some companies will allow their employees to decide what they want to learn; others develop internal learning programs and partner with learning institutions to help their employees grow both personally and professionally. By embedding a culture of coaching, teaching and role modeling, a company says that education and ongoing skills and knowledge advancement matters.

This section explores how Runway East combines employee personal development with L&D and how Ballouniversity was created to develop courses and foster an environment of education and enrichment at Ballou.

1. Runway East

Natasha Guerra, CEO of Runway East, has built a team of 30 young and hungry millennials who operate five startup coworking spaces in the UK. Based on the feedback she received from her team about the need for more learning and development initiatives, and combined with the request to develop career paths, she decided to roll out a Personal Development Plan (PDP) program for the company. "We've grown quickly over the last 18 months. As a leadership team we felt that we needed to stabilize the foundations of the business by gaining a deeper understanding of our team, their strengths, weaknesses and motivations while giving them a learning and development plan to work toward."

The company ran a PDP workshop for the management team, as no one had experienced running a PDP before. "The workshop's objective was for the management team to come away with a clear understanding of the PDP process, for them to be confident on how to lead a PDP, and set S.M.A.R.T goals (Specific, Measurable, Achievable, Realistic and Timely). It was also important to understand how to follow up from the initial PDP and how to help coach their reports along the process."

As with every new initiative, there is a learning curve, and PDPs can be challenging as not everybody is used to doing a deep dive into their strengths and weaknesses or their short-, mid-, or long-term goals. "I am happy with what we achieved with the first PDP session. It's important that the management team use the PDPs as a baseline during their monthly GAD (Give A Damn) one-to-one meetings to ensure that their team members are on track with their PDPs, or if not, what we need to do about it."

2. Ballou

Colette Ballou, founder and CEO of the PR firm Ballou, decided to set up a learning and development program for her team a couple of years ago. To demonstrate the value of *A commitment to bring creative solutions to problems*, Ballou didn't just offer her team many training opportunities, she created Ballouniversity. Ballou said that "Ballouniversity is an investment in multiple areas of L&D, raising the skill level across the company, sharing knowledge across the three offices, offering a progression path for each of our team members, while also codifying our culture. We surveyed the team about the skills they needed to develop and the knowledge they wanted to learn, and we spoke with the management team and board of directors about what skills we should be teaching to further the company."

The Ballouniversity program offers 10 courses each year, in each of its offices, on a revolving basis. The program also incorporates an office exchange program: four people attend the program from the office where it's being held, and two people attend from the other two offices. Each course involves learning about and developing essential next-level skills such as presentation skills and perfecting the new business process. "Attending the courses help employees learn, develop, understand how to live the values, and gain the skills they need to succeed and be promoted. I've always felt that if a team member is not promotable, it's not just them—it's also a failure of management."

VI. HOW YOU REACT TO CRISES, CRITICAL SITUATIONS AND FAILURE TO LIVE THE VALUES

The way you respond to critical incidents, issues, failures, unpredicted changes and crises will reveal your underlying values, attitude and perspective. A crisis like the COVID-19 pandemic can be especially significant for the development and strengthening of your culture. Typically, the stronger your people's emotional involvement during the crisis, the greater the intensity of learning. If you show your team the values being lived, they become deeply integrated into the culture during these trying times. You will do tremendous and lasting damage to the culture you have built if you don't live up to the values during such times.

This section discusses how Adaptive Insights' leaders used their failures to learn what they were doing wrong and move the business forward, then I look at how Guidion solved a transparency issue between management and the rest of the employees.

1. Adaptive Insights

Culture-driven companies use failure and other crises as learning opportunities. Tom Bogan, CEO of Adaptive Insights, used his team's failure to hit their target as a tool to reinforce the values of transparency and accountability with the team. After Bogan took over as CEO, Adaptive Insights went through a couple of tough quarters, where the company failed to meet its targets. Rather than try to sugar-coat the failures, Bogan dug into the issues and tried to find what could be learned to help the company going forward. "We shared what we missed, why we thought it had happened, and what we planned to do to get back on track. It's not easy to do this—the conventional wisdom is that you shouldn't share bad news because you'll frighten people and leave. People can take difficult news if you have built the right foundation, and the team understands and appreciates transparency. In the long run, it builds more trust and loyalty."

Bogan's next step was to focus on developing personal accountability. He introduced a process in which everyone would have goals and share their results and performance against those goals in public forums. "We aimed to set a precedent where people would proactively volunteer that they missed their goals or didn't get something done." Bogan knew that as a leader, to do this effectively, you must start by holding yourself accountable, so that's where he began. "We had some difficult off-site meetings, where the leadership team would sometimes say that we were too tough, to which I'd reply that we weren't tough enough because we weren't asking the hard questions. We don't want people to come in and give us a bunch of spin. That's not going to solve any problems. Instead, we've really got to understand where we are at any one point in time."

After a couple of challenging sessions, the broader management team really started taking responsibility and began to ask tough questions of their team. "Now our product leader isn't afraid of asking a hard question out in the field, and our field leaders aren't afraid to ask hard questions of the product team. Nobody is perfect, and we still have work to do, but I think we're far better than we were a few years ago."

By demonstrating and reinforcing the values of transparency and accountability, Bogan created the right environment and success for Workday to acquire the company for $1.5 billion in 2018.

2. Guidion

Maarten Roerink, the former CEO of Guidion, the Amsterdam-based Craftsman as a Service platform, realized that the company's leadership team was failing to live two of the company's values, *Transparency* and the *Rapid distribution of information,* as the result of a question from an employee. Roerink decided to start a new business tradition by having an employee sit in on the Monday management meeting. "This came about when I was asked what I did as the CEO and what was discussed in the management meetings, which had always taken place behind closed doors and were never reported on." Roerink recognized a serious failure to live the *Transparency* and the *Rapid distribution of information* values at the leadership level, and that there was a potential problem of distrust developing around what his staff imagined was being discussed in the meetings. "People were naturally assuming all sorts of things—some negative—that could easily have hindered our progress as a business." The role of the employee who joins the Monday meeting is to listen, give feedback to the leadership team, write up a transcript of the meeting and post it on Sonar, Guidion's internal culture management platform. "Within a few minutes of the meeting ending, everybody knows what we've been discussing and why it's relevant. It's a great learning experience for the employee, and every six months a new person is chosen to sit in on the meetings. This way we, as senior management, are also truly accountable, in that we don't say one thing and do another."

Inviting employees into management meetings cut this failure off at the pass, demonstrating and reinforcing the *Transparency* and *Rapid distribution of information* values.

IN CONCLUSION...

The six primary embedding mechanisms can be summarized as how a leader rewards and recognizes performance, attracts and retains talent, measures and prioritizes, makes investments, develops their people and reacts to crises within their organization. The examples in this chapter demonstrate that there are many ways to strengthen your culture through the six embedding mechanisms.

It is your responsibility to understand which embedding mechanisms are relevant to you and if, through alignment with the company values, those mechanisms encourage positive culture development. If there is misalignment, the team will be confused about what the leader truly values and make their own interpretation.

Few leaders deliberately monitor how they act and behave as managers inside their company. Most may think that no one is watching, but they are wrong. Your teams are watching closely. The six primary embedding mechanisms give you and your leadership team the framework to become deliberate about embedding your culture in the right way.

Chapter 9

Feedback and Proactive Learning Environments

"Always keep learning. You stop doing useful things if you don't learn…, especially if you have had some initial success. It becomes even more critical that you have the learning 'bit' always switched on."
– Satya Nadella, CEO, Microsoft

A highly effective culture needs to be simultaneously a paradigm of stability *and* adaptability. It might at first sound oxymoronic or counterintuitive. Still, aspects of a culture must demonstrate stability to ensure that your team feels secure, united and safe, enabling them to work without adding undue anxiety. Other aspects of the culture must develop the capability in the individuals and hence the company to be flexible in the face of regular, yet unexpected, change.

The culture-driven CEO understands that learning is equivalent to building that flexibility for the business, and therefore invests in it wholeheartedly and unstintingly. A proactive learning environment combines each team member's personal need for constant development with the organization's need to be able to learn and adapt to the ongoing changes in the external environment.

In our volatile, uncertain, complex and ambiguous business environment, the key realization for a culture-driven leader is that they can't and won't know everything—and neither will the team. It's impossible. However, what *is* possible is the capability to continuously increase the individual and collective knowledge of your team and company. Proactive learning companies approach problem-solving as a shared search for solutions.

A company that does proactive learning is also fanatic about feedback. Handling feedback well is another way to show you have a proactive learning mentality. In these companies, feedback is treated like a muscle to be developed and strengthened. This encourages and rewards team members who ask for and then learn from that feedback. Culture-driven leaders know that giving and receiving feedback is an inherent and inescapable part of leadership. They understand that feedback is a central ingredient in providing effective mentorship and growth and that it is also vital in facilitating innovation, productivity and progress.

Culture-driven leaders also know that people struggle with the giving of or the receiving of feedback…or both. Therefore, these leaders think deeply about feedback and incorporate it within the teams they lead effectively. They are conscious of their colleagues' unique personalities and how they can most effectively receive feedback.

Intelligently incorporating feedback as a practice or other learning and development programs requires thought and reflective practice: trying something, reflecting on what works and iterating. Culture-driven leaders deliberately create a work environment where the team can experiment, learn and improve through trial and error. Such a leader knows that failures are valuable lessons and stepping stones to success.

Culture-driven leaders deliberately create a work environment where the team can experiment, learn and improve through trial and error.

This chapter explores the different approaches to learning and development that the culture-driven leaders have taken to develop proactive learning environments. Evonomix invests in staff skills and career development while accounting for it as investing in long-term success. Learnerbly trains its staff how to give and receive feedback.

LiveRamp set up an L&D function and trains managers to be better leaders and models of the company culture. CharlieHR integrates feedback into weekly stand-up meetings. Hotjar invests in individual learning, giving all employees unlimited membership to the online learning platform Udemy, an annual learning budget and a Kindle Paperwhite. SalesLoft has developed a high-feedback culture, which has allowed it to do away with performance reviews completely.

1. Evonomix

Evonomix CEO Mihai Bocai realizes that continual investment in his team is critical if, in a highly competitive market, his company is to stand any chance of success over the long-term. He set the scene by saying that "Our main challenge is finding the right talent. We have a strong pipeline of customers and our own internal opportunities; we are simply desperate to find the right people. It's a very challenging market to operate in." Bocai explains that Evonomix offers market rate salary packages, while in some cases competitors are offering candidates double Evonomix's base salary. "Our approach is this: if money is the only thing that you believe will bring you happiness, then we are not the right place for you to work. At Evonomix we are all about self-development, learning and growing. Over the last two years we have found that our people stay with us not because of money, but because they are learning, growing and developing themselves, and trusting our technical view of the future."

Evonomix works with employees to develop a personalized career plan that starts at the onboarding stage of their journey. Evonomix has created a development program that covers understanding the company basics such as its values, brand and mission through digital skills training, leadership development, and current and future job-related skills. The program helps get new team members up to speed quickly, demonstrates the company's ongoing commitment to people development and the long-term opportunities of working at Evonomix. One of the job requirements at Evonomix is that each employee must sign up for—and pass—an internationally recognized certification in their field of expertise every year, with the longer-term aim of developing a team of subject matter experts. The company offers unlimited training on anything if employees who complete the training share what they have learned with the team.

Due to the competitive nature of the local talent market, Bocai has gone one step further to attract talent as early as possible in the supply chain by developing training and development initiatives with the local university in Constanța, Romania. Bocai explained to me, "We decided to move down the talent supply chain and have invested in training people while they are still at university."

Bocai is differentiating his company from the competition by focusing on learning and development and creating an environment where developing subject matter experts expect to join the company. He doesn't feel compelled to join the salary price war to stand out. As Bocai said, "Our main challenge is finding and retaining the right talent and these programs differentiate us from the competition."

2. Learnerbly

Learnerbly is a VC-backed tech company that helps curate the best learning opportunities for companies to help accelerate their people's growth and development. COO Melissa Andrada decided that to really live the company's *Practice heartfelt, radical candor* value, Learnerbly needed to get everyone on the team comfortable giving and receiving feedback. So, she designed and implemented the Learnerbly Feedback program. According to Andrada, "We ran an employee survey to diagnose where our people were in terms of their comfort in giving and receiving feedback. In the survey, we asked questions like, 'How comfortable do you feel about giving and receiving feedback, on a scale of one to ten?' 'What's been your most impactful feedback moment and why?' We wanted people to really think critically about feedback from the outset."

Andrada also led a training session where everyone described their preferred ways of receiving feedback. Two types of feedback emerged: behavioral feedback and project-based feedback. "While project-based feedback is less personal and most people didn't care how that was being given, it's a lot harder to hear if someone gives feedback about your body language, confidence or weird idiosyncrasy you have." She found that many of her team members preferred to have this kind of feedback communicated in person and in private.

During this internal training session Andrada provided a forum for discussion to help people air out some of their fears and challenges. The forum captured how different types of people like to give and receive feedback, which the company documented and made easily accessible in an open Google Doc. "It was fascinating understanding how the introverts and extroverts on our team prefer to receive feedback. For example, the more introverted types want to be able to read the feedback first and then are happy to talk about it; the more extroverted are happy to just talk about it from the offset."

To supplement the internal training, Andrada brought in an external training company to run a session on productive feedback conversations. "The framework that they introduced is about context setting, fact-based communication, how to ask the right questions and defining actions, which really helped the new joiners get up to speed on the type of feedback culture we wanted to develop within the company."

Learnerbly has a business rhythm, which includes stand-up meetings on Monday and weekly retrospectives on Fridays, and they have a regular cadence of learning sessions. Andrada explained, "We are incorporating feedback into the things we already do as part of the business's rhythm so that it doesn't feel like we're launching a whole new initiative. We specifically integrated a feedback session into the Friday retrospectives. We ask people to give someone on the team a piece of feedback, and we are looking at ways to build it into our Monday stand-ups."

Through the surveys and internal and external training sessions, the company invests money, effort and time toward creating an environment where everyone at Learnerbly can give and receive feedback effectively. This demonstrates to the team that the leadership is serious about the value of *Practicing heartfelt, radical candor*.

3. LiveRamp

Anneka Gupta, President of LiveRamp, the SaaS identity resolution provider, has helped build the company from 25 people to over 1,000 in under a decade. The company started to build a dedicated learning and development (L&D) function about two and a half years ago, and the team has developed a range of options for employees to participate in. As Gupta described, "We support a lot of different forms of learning, from working with executive coaches who will do individual coaching and group sessions with different teams, to our people attending conferences and doing courses relevant to their personal development plan."

When I spoke with her, Gupta had been thinking about getting first-time inexperienced middle managers to further promote the living and owning of the values into their teams, which is one big challenge in a larger organization. "As the business expanded, we realized that top-level leaders were living and promoting the culture, but we needed to get our middle management to start to view their leadership roles and decision-making process through the lens of living the culture. We realized they needed help with understanding how to lead through the values, how to model the right behavior, and how to instill that behavior into their teams.

"We built out a leadership and culture training program for middle managers. It has been invaluable in improving our managers' abilities and promoting and living the values down into the organization."

One of LiveRamp's values is *We empower people*. By offering leadership and culture training to the mid-level managers, the company demonstrates how committed it is to ensure that all of its culture can be understood, lived and promoted at all levels of the organization.

4. CharlieHR

At CharlieHR, cofounder and Chairman Rob O'Donovan fiercely advocates radical candor, which calls for honest and straightforward communication. As O'Donovan explained, "We have a meeting every Monday called 'Focus and Feedback'; it's like a regular stand-up meeting with a twist." During the stand-up each team member discusses what their focus will be in the coming week, and then they share the feedback they have received. How this works is, before every meeting, each member approaches someone with whom they worked that past week and asks for their feedback, which they will share at Monday's meeting.

O'Donovan makes sure to lead by example, as he believes that the company culture applies more to him than everyone else. He asks for and accepts his team's feedback as valuable input, then actively works to improve his behavior accordingly. "The feedback that I received from my colleagues and that I had to communicate to the team at our recent stand-up is that I can be unapproachable when I am swamped and working toward a deadline. The reason for this is I'm trying to get as much done as possible. The team doesn't feel comfortable in approaching me for help or advice when I am that busy. It happened most recently before my vacation, and it's something that I will need to work on."

Being open to feedback means embracing vulnerability, and, as O'Donovan noted above, that can be scary. An increased trust can offset this fear. "New joiners struggle with this process at first," he pointed out, "but it really is beneficial. It builds an environment of honesty, where people can talk openly about something they are struggling with. This builds emotional resilience in the team." In most companies, if you merely ask for feedback, you won't get the actionable feedback you want or need; you need to proactively create an environment such that the feedback people end up giving and receiving is valuable and worthwhile.

5. Hotjar

"The main feedback we see takes on the form of requests for guidance about what to learn," said CEO of Hotjar David Darmanin. "Generally, what I answer to that is, if you're looking for someone to tell you what to learn, that is not the ideal place to be. Learning is something that you take your own initiative on, where you create your own path. That makes it difficult for anyone to tell you, 'Go learn this, go do that.'" A sense of direction and a thirst for knowledge, he added, "should be part of the job already."

Darmanin says that he and the team wish to instill more learning and development within the company, and the company's initiatives are encouraged by a generous L&D budget for each department. His advice is based on three of his principles regarding Hotjar's proactive learning process.

1. **Invest in individual learning.** Hotjar gives everyone in the team a Kindle Paperwhite as well as unlimited membership to Udemy so that they can go and learn anything they desire. The company also provides individual (annual) development budgets for everyone, which is currently $555 per person. Each week, the team hosts a demo showing how people are using their personal developmental budget (buying books, taking courses, etc.), and this is shared with the rest of the team.

2. **Allow departments to choose.** The leaders of each department are most familiar with what their team members require and desire in terms of learning and development, so Darmanin believes that they should have the liberty to decide what events to attend, what learning initiatives to chase, and so forth.

3. **Encourage sharing and networking.** "There's a lot of value in hearing people share what they're doing, so we create numerous opportunities for that to happen within Hotjar," Darmanin said, emphasizing the importance of participating at various learning seminars and events the company holds internally and encourages its people to attend externally. There's an added bonus, of course: "They're also a great opportunity to get to know your teammates and for networking."

6. SalesLoft

SalesLoft has developed a culture without performance reviews. "I do not believe in the annual performance review," Christine Kaszubski Chief People Officer explained. "I don't believe in performance review ratings. When you're having a conversation with an employee and you're providing them with feedback, the message is what matters. It's not, 'You are a three, you are a four, you are a "meets expectations," you're an "exceed expectations,"' which is what many of the leading companies still use. So, I completely removed that." "In place of typical performance reviews, SalesLoft has developed a high feedback culture," Kaszubski continued. "We teach radical candor, which is based on Kim Scott's excellent book *Radical Candor*, and we live by that." To oversimplify slightly, at SalesLoft this means communicating honestly, with respect and setting clear expectations.

Instead of having an annual review the teams have daily stand-ups and weekly meetings; managers and direct reports have weekly one-to-ones; there are quarterly OKRs, quarterly feedback sessions, two biannual merit review processes and the 6 Ps of Fit, which is an evaluation process SalesLoft has been testing and will be introduced across the company later this year.

"The 6 Ps of Fit program we have developed centers around people's personal needs, preferences and personal goals. At 90 days into the role, and as part of the annual merit review, instead of looking at whether people accomplished specific projects, they will be asked how they feel about their fit within the job and organization. It's about taking the whole human self into consideration," Kaszubski explained. "Because we are growing so fast, not just in size but in skill set, I want to make sure that we're continuing to stay on track with fit. We want to make sure that we're keeping our top talent. Our low turnover rate is not enough. I don't want to keep people in the same job; I want them to continue learning more, do more and become more. I want to make sure that we're keeping up with what they're looking for and what the organization needs." This holistic approach really does make the typical annual performance review, where a manager meets with the individuals in their team once a year, seem pretty basic.

SalesLoft doesn't take a linear approach to providing people with a "career ladder" either. "It's more like a career jungle gym because there will be jobs we create next year that we haven't even thought about yet," Kaszubski explained. She aims to enable the company's future leaders by creating core competencies and skill sets so that when an opportunity comes up, they're ready to take it. What those opportunities look like will become apparent in time.

Developing those skill sets happens in lots of ways at SalesLoft. A bespoke in-house L&D program called LoftEd launched in late 2019 provides access to LinkedIn Learning and individual development plans. The company offers Lunch & Learn sessions on subjects like Radical Candor and Patrick Lencioni's *Five Dysfunctions of a Team*. Leaders are offered a robust training and development program called Lead: a two-day manager boot camp where they learn the tactical and functional approach to being a leader at SalesLoft, followed by monthly training sessions for six months. Leaders cover topics such as high-impact coaching, situational leadership, strategy and implementation.

Ongoing, all employees are offered a tuition reimbursement program of over $5,000 per Lofter per year. Kaszubski believes this creates the equivalent of a curriculum that is totally tailored to each individual.

IN CONCLUSION...

A culture of learning is characterized by leadership who embrace mistakes as learning experiences, thereby building trust and encouraging feedback, and creating a value system around learning. Although proactive learning provides a tremendous ROI when correctly implemented, it isn't a strategy that has to cost you excess time or money. You can always begin by implementing an inexpensive and straightforward internal strategy that can facilitate feedback, skill-building and innovation regardless of your company's size or industry. These action points can be:

- Replace or supplement performance evaluations with regular feedback sessions.
- Embed feedback initiatives into your weekly/monthly meetings.
- Develop a Personal Development Plan for each team member.
- Talk about (and follow up on) everyone's learning plan at your weekly/monthly meetings.
- Invite experts to share their experiences through storytelling, providing your team with a more easily accessible source of input and inspiration.

- Encourage senior leaders to hold internal workshops, seminars, or informal lunch-and-learn opportunities to transfer knowledge and foster connections between veteran and fledgling team members.
- In preparation for rapid growth, start to build the mentality in the organization of doing jobs that haven't been created yet.

If you have the budget and start to experience rapid growth, you might want to consider the following:

- Organize an external trainer to help develop your company's feedback muscle specifically.
- Build a dedicated L&D (Learning & Development) team or a bespoke L&D program.
- Create a curriculum that is tailored to each individual.
- Give your people the budget and responsibility for their L&D.

Chapter 10

Trust, Transparency and Psychological Safety

"We deliberately try to drive the company toward an environment of transparency so that people are able and empowered to make decisions on the information they have at hand." – Maarten Roerink, CEO, Guidion

Take a moment to consider the context of our global economy and marketplace. Studies have shown that American consumers distrust businesses more than ever before, a fact that's likely backed up by your own convictions. The Corporate Perception Indicator survey reported that only 36 percent of Americans saw corporations as a "source of hope."

Why such distrust? Certainly, there is the perception of greedy, misleading and deceitful institutions that contributed to the global economic crash more than a decade ago. From United Airlines' forcible removal of a passenger, to Samsung's charges of bribery and hiding assets overseas. From the sexual harassment scandals at Fox News to the Harvey Weinstein scandal, to the criminal probes and unethical culture of Uber to WeWork's founder woes, distrust in business is at an all-time high.

Transparency in business, which goes hand in hand with trust, is something that has become more precious and coveted. Culture-driven leaders who practice and demonstrate transparency understand that it is not a buzzword; to treat it that way would mean to fall into the trap of reinforcing distrust instead of eradicating it.

In essence, transparency is "clear, unhindered honesty" in the way that a person does business; BusinessDictionary.com defines it as the "lack of hidden agendas and conditions, accompanied by the availability of full information required for collaboration, cooperation and collective decision-making."

Transparency is a word that embodies the highest ethics of a company: honesty, respect, open and timely communication and authenticity. These values in turn enable trust and cooperation, which understandably, in turn, promote higher performance, greater quality, and a happier and more united company culture that extends from the inside out, impacting and inspiring employees and customers alike. It ensures a win-win for the company and the type of client who rallies around it.

Transparency means telling the truth to employees even when it's bad news, and being open to the outside world.

Transparency means telling the truth to employees even when it's bad news and being open to the outside world. When you're open about your financials, your hiring practices and how you conduct yourself as a business, people will trust you and be drawn to you because they know that you will always tell them the truth, regardless of whether it's favorable or negative, and you won't come up with unexpected or unpleasant surprises.

In 2011, Google started a multi-year study called Project Aristotle[8] to understand how to build the perfect team.

They studied various configurations of people to see under what conditions a high-performing team emerged, and they were surprised that a team's propensity to thrive did not rest on whether the group consisted of the right blend of extroversion and introversion, whether there was the right mix of diversity, or even whether the team was made up of highly competent players. The researchers stumbled upon a concept that finally shed light on the critical factor that determined the extent to which a team would perform at a high level: the level of psychological safety present in the system.

The term "psychological safety" was coined by Harvard Professor Amy Edmondson in the 1990s. Edmondson defines it as a "shared belief held by members of a team that the team is safe for interpersonal risk-taking," and "sense of confidence that the team will not embarrass, reject or punish someone for speaking up." When psychological safety is present, people sense that they can voice challenging, potentially unwanted opinions and give difficult, hard-to-hear feedback to colleagues without it negatively impacting their careers. When people feel safe, they take risks, push boundaries of creativity and voice ideas, perspectives and opinions that they might otherwise keep quiet. This can have a tangible impact on the direction a business takes. Organizations that are struggling to generate genuinely innovative ideas might want to take note.

What Project Aristotle has taught people within Google is that no one wants to put on a "work face" when they get to the office. No one wants to leave part of their personality and inner life at home. People want to be fully present at work, to feel "psychologically safe." We must know that we can be free enough, sometimes, to share the things that scare us without fear of recrimination. We must be able to talk about what is messy or sad, to have hard conversations with colleagues who are driving us crazy. We can't be focused just on efficiency. We want to know that work is more than just labor.

In organizations where psychological safety is lacking, people are unsurprisingly on edge, guarded and defensive. They end up "hiding, lying and faking" their way through the day, as they call it at Next Jump, a culture-driven technology company and Deliberately Developmental Organization (DDO).

Consciously creating a culture where psychological safety is present should, therefore, be a priority for founders and leaders who want to build companies that thrive. In psychologically safe teams, people trust each other across the organization: leaders and managers believe that their people will get the work done that they need to get done, and their reports trust that they can bring their ideas and passion to the table and that their best interest is held high. When trust is present, the need to micromanage falls away, which frees up a manager's time and attention while simultaneously empowering their direct reports.

In this chapter I look at six companies that are working to strengthen trust and transparency. Unbounce publishes an annual blog post where the CEO shares the company's financials even if they don't have to. The

Emarsys CEO discusses how transparency has helped the team live their *We embrace tomorrow* value. Algolia learns that total transparency isn't always achievable as the company scales. Headliner realizes that its culture is not as transparent as it would like. Thread comes to grips with candor and trust. And at Audiobooks, two executives whose actions were not promoting trust were terminated.

1. Unbounce

Rick Perreault, CEO of Unbounce, described to me the positive effects that transparency and open communication have on his business. "Take our value of transparency: we are and always have been transparent in terms of the business financials. There is nothing off the table when it comes to the numbers. We have always been very open about where the business stands so that our team can make more informed decisions." Sharing the financials via the blog is a great example of how living the transparency value can have a positive effect on the business. "Hiring is very competitive in Vancouver and we have had situations where candidates have chosen Unbounce over other companies because we deliver on our transparency value in this way."

Perreault described how this transparency policy starts the day a new employee joins the company. "I do a presentation on the history of the company and where we are headed. There is a presentation on the financial state of the business and at the end of the day I meet with the new joiners for an hour so that they can ask me anything about the company. If the new joiners make it through the probation period, I will meet again with the whole cohort to welcome them onboard and answer any additional questions they may have." This is full availability and authenticity. Perreault invests this time with his new employees because he wants every one of his 150 employees to know that they can knock on his door at any time if they have something to talk about. "This helps create an open environment for open communication—if you ask the CEO anything and talk to the CEO about anything, then you can ask questions or talk to anyone else in the company at any time."

2. Emarsys

Emarsys CEO Ohad Hecht discussed how transparency has helped the team live their *We embrace tomorrow* value. Hecht explained that change is happening throughout the organization constantly, and everyone says that they like change, but no one actually likes it that much. "When change comes, people usually sit back and wait to see what happens. They don't lean into it or embrace it. So, the question was how we make sure that our people are leaning in, moving forward and opening their hands to the opportunities, rather than closing them." Hecht decided to set up a weekly company-wide meeting and really double down on being transparent, which would allow everyone in the company to understand how the leadership team was perceiving and dealing with those changes. "We have weekly meetings in every country where we are fully transparent about the current state of the business. We tell employees everything that is happening in the company; we don't hide anything. In terms of the changes we see and how we believe they will impact the business, we tell people what we believe in and why, what answers we have and which ones we don't, what we are doing and what will happen if we don't."

This transparent approach has been very effective in getting the people in the company to *embrace tomorrow*. According to Hecht there is a much better understanding of the current state of the business at any particular time, why the company needs to make the changes the leadership team is proposing, and how employees can embrace and find opportunities in the changes. "Our people have been more proactive about anticipating and communicating changes in their teams and departments since the new approach was instated."

3. Algolia

Up until May 2018, Algolia, an enterprise search SaaS company, had been transparent across the board with everything it could possibly be transparent about. Cofounder Nicolas Dessaigne explained, "When Julian and I started the company we had nothing to hide and when we were recruiting our initial teammates, we were essentially adding co-owners to the business. Our approach was that we are all owners of the company and we are all in the same team, so why would we hide anything from each other or anyone else we brought into the company?" The founders recognized that an open and transparent approach to running the business was a real differentiator for the company and they set out to keep the company as transparent as possible for as long as possible.

"It's not that easy, though," Dessaigne said. "It isn't trivial to be fully transparent as you scale a business globally. When HR issues crop up for example, you can't be fully transparent because it's actually disrespectful to the people involved to be totally transparent. When you are fundraising, you are not going to be transparent during the process itself because people can easily interpret signals in the wrong way." Privacy laws of various jurisdictions where Algolia operates can also get in the way. In fact in May 2018, the decision was made, due mainly to privacy issues, to discontinue their approach of making employee remuneration fully transparent. As the company grew, the team had to adapt and respond to the realities of the market dynamics in different regions.

A change in approach to something as significant as transparency around employee remuneration can have a negative effect on the morale and attitude of the team. Dessaigne said, "What normally happens is people assume the worst when you take something away or hide something that they had full access to. Because we had worked so hard on it, we had a lot of trust and goodwill in place. If you have trust in place, your people are going to assume the best. As a leader, people may disagree with some of your decisions, but if your people trust you, they will assume you have good intentions."

Algolia makes all their financial and other company data (excluding salaries and legally sensitive information) available to employees via an employee portal. Dessaigne said, "The surprising thing for me is as soon as people have access to the data, they hardly look at it. It's not like we are a listed company where there are changes happening to the share price every day; our people know it's there and they know they can access it when they want to."

If you scale your business to hundreds of employees in international offices the way Algolia has done, you have to work hard to live up to high standards of transparency, balancing the expectations of your team with the legal and privacy requirements of the different jurisdictions in which you operate. The key to Algolia's relatively seamless transition to a slightly less transparent company was the goodwill that the founders had built through the trust and ownership mentality they had developed from day one.

4. Headliner

Stan McLeod, cofounder and CEO of Headliner, a company that connects event planners with musicians, bands and DJs to perform at events, noted that cultivating a transparent work culture is a constant challenge. His company upholds *transparency, freedom, self-expression* and *open communication* as core values on which the business operates. "People who have previously been in challenging or different cultures don't necessary get ours, especially in the beginning, because they're used to something else." One time, he and his leadership team tried to be more accommodating to their customers who worked odd hours and wanted the ability to make bookings during evenings and weekends, so they introduced an idea that the team needed to become more involved in customer support. During this discussion, nobody on the team disagreed or brought up any questions or concerns; McLeod assumed everyone was happy with the arrangement. A couple of days later, he heard how two team members mentioned that it didn't feel "right or fair."

"What frustrated me," McLeod explained, "is that we are trying to build an environment of transparency and open communication, yet some team members don't bring their concerns up when we discuss a business initiative. It turned out, once I explained it in more detail and it was understood, that they were more than happy to pitch in and help. Looking back on this, there were two issues: I didn't communicate in detail the context for introducing shared customer support, and they didn't feel the trust to bring the issue or misunderstanding up immediately." Pushing past his frustration that these employees hadn't spoken out during the discussion, McLeod grasped this as a major indicator that the culture *wasn't* as transparent as he thought it was, and this became a turning point and learning opportunity.

"For our business to succeed, we need that type of misunderstanding to be dealt with in real time," McLeod added. "People will step back into the default negative culture that they're used to—where they were told what to do and couldn't question it— if we allow them to. As leaders, it is our job to make sure that it doesn't happen, and this is something we are actively working harder on now." Headliner has put programs in place to encourage its people to be comfortable challenging the leadership at the point of delivery of the information, especially if they feel that communication is not clear. McLeod continued, "We want to foster a culture of transparency where everyone is listened to, understood and respected. I care about working as a culture, not as a business."

5. Thread

Thread CEO Kieran O'Neill understands that a culture of full transparency can initially be a little scary, especially for teams who are used to less transparent mindsets and business behaviors. "Candor is the hardest of our values to live up to, because in England there is a societal culture of being polite and somewhat indirect. It's also harder because it's the one value that carries a form of personal risk if it's not reciprocated. If an intern says to the CEO, 'Hey, I think this could've gone better,' the upside of the interaction for the intern is small. The best outcome is that the CEO thinks the intern is great for giving feedback. The downside is getting fired or getting blackballed if the CEO doesn't actually practice what they preach and takes offense to what was said."

In order to promote candor, O'Neill emphasized that it's essential to invest in cultivating a culture of trust where people are able—and comfortable—to communicate openly and honesty. "It's not something that happens overnight, nor is it a mentality that comes easily for everyone." Trust is earned, and as O'Neill put it, "Trust is the foundation of a strong culture, just as it is the foundation of every successful relationship."

6. Audiobooks

The absence of trust can have numerous negative cumulative effects on your business. Sanjay Singhal, Canadian tech entrepreneur and cofounder and former CEO of Audiobooks, came to realize that he had a trust issue in his executive team after reading *The Five Dysfunctions of a Team: A Leadership Fable* by Patrick Lencioni. The book helped him realize that there was a serious absence of trust at the executive level in his company and in order to restore this trust, he had to remove two executives. Singhal said, "Any absence of trust lies with team members being unable to show their weaknesses; to be vulnerable and open with one another. The absence of trust is a huge waste of time and energy as team members focus on defensive behaviors and are reluctant to ask for help from, or assist, each other." Singhal knew that he had to create an environment where team members could, as he put it, "Overcome this dysfunction by sharing experiences, demonstrating credibility and developing strong insight into the unique characteristics of other team members." By removing the team members who were not promoting trust, Singhal was rebuilding the psychological safety of the organization. "I had been unaware of the trust issues we had at the senior executive level. We now have a much stronger, more cohesive executive team and a happier company."

IN CONCLUSION...

Many companies have not grasped the importance of transparency as a meaningful competitive advantage, especially in the current market. But those companies that do build a culture on open communication, respectful relationships and transparent interactions are the companies that enjoy excellent cultures and customer and employee loyalty—and all the productive and profitable results that naturally ensue.

Some of the actionable lessons to build a work environment of trust and transparency from this chapter include:

- Trust takes time to earn but can be lost in seconds. You can build up "trust goodwill" in your organization over time by demonstrating it constantly, and you can use some of this goodwill to ease the effect of uncomfortable decisions.
- Decide what's on and off the table when it comes to transparency. Be specific in your communication about anything that needs to be kept confidential, in some cases by law and in others to protect employees and the company.
- Foster a transparent environment by making sure that people are listened to, understood, respected and feel psychologically safe.
- Put programs in place to encourage your people to be comfortable challenging the leadership at the point of delivery of the information.
- Remove anyone who propagates an absence of trust among employees.

- When hiring for transparency and trust, develop values-based interview questions that evaluate a candidate's empathy, openness, honesty, integrity, directness and ability to give and receive feedback.

Chapter 11

Diversity and Inclusion

"Diversity is being invited to the party; inclusion is being asked to dance." – Verna Myers, cultural change catalyst

"Many successful companies regard D&I as a source of competitive advantage. For some, it's a matter of social justice, corporate social responsibility, or even regulatory compliance. For others, it's essential to their growth strategy."
– McKinsey, "Delivering Through Diversity[9]" report, 2018.

Diversity and inclusion (D&I) have massively come to the fore in recent years, the consensus being that they are both critical factors for businesses to address for a host of reasons, as highlighted by McKinsey.

With so much pressure on startup founders to grow, hit KPIs and close the next funding round, D&I is not even a blip on the radar for most founders. For some founders D&I feels like a somewhat obligatory area to address and their approach is to get to it when they have more time. For other founders it is part and parcel of the company they are building, who they are and how they operate, and as a result, it is something they focus on from the outset. Viewed through this lens D&I can be compared to culture development, and I believe that D&I's time has arrived.

Inclusion is described in the Cambridge Dictionary as the "act of including someone or something as part of a group." A culture of inclusion ensures that everyone in the organization is heard and considered and feels empowered to contribute. It allows employees from all backgrounds and walks of life to achieve their fullest potential. An *inclusive* culture is one that accepts, values and sees as a strength the differences we all bring to the table.

In its 2020 "Getting to Equal" report (called "The Hidden Value of Culture Makers"), Accenture finds that there is a large gap between what leaders think is going on and what employees say is happening on the ground. Two thirds of leaders surveyed by Accenture (68 percent) feel they create inclusive empowering environments—in which employees can be themselves, raise concerns and innovate without fear of failure— but just one third (36 percent) of employees agree. This gap is due to the fact that, while diversity is more straightforward to measure, inclusion is a much more subjective target.

Diversity is when different ethnicities, ages, genders, abilities, nationalities, socioeconomic statuses, etc. are well represented within a company. The group is diverse if a wide enough variety of groups are represented. You should not seek diversity for diversity's sake. When discussing diversity, I am not talking about diverse people who cannot do the job or do not match your company's values—these requirements are fundamental to the success of the business. Also, you cannot expect diversity to just work. Bringing together a group of people with divergent ways of thinking and working is bound to generate some conflict. For diversity to be beneficial, you must have defined the company's vision, mission, core values and expected behaviors. A strong, functional culture creates an environment where difference is appreciated and generates brilliance rather than unproductive difficulty. A diverse team will not be like you or think like you, but will challenge you, will push you to innovate and understand diverse markets, and will be capable of viewing the world of solutions, problems, opportunities and threats in a fresh and different way.

There is a lot of talk about "the business case" for diversity, and the statistically significant correlation between diverse leadership teams and financial outperformance, reported by McKinsey, is often pointed out. For example, companies in the top-quartile for gender diversity on executive teams are 21 percent more likely to outperform others on profitability. The highest-performing companies on both profitability and diversity have more women in line roles (i.e., revenue-generating) than in staff roles (i.e., non-revenue-generating) on their executive teams. This tracks for ethnic and cultural diversity, too: those in the top quartile are 33 percent more likely to be industry leaders in terms of their profitability. At the opposite end of the scale, the correlation continues: companies in the bottom quartile for both gender and ethnic and cultural diversity were 29 percent less likely to demonstrate above-average profitability than all the other companies on the data set (McKinsey 2018).

In this chapter I look at how Jellyvision treats D&I as a muscle that needs constant training and at how Periscope Data focuses on inclusion before diversity. We see how Algolia increased the percentage of under-represented minority employees from 4 percent to 11 percent and how LiveRamp makes D&I the responsibility of everyone in the company.

1. Algolia

Nicolas Dessaigne, cofounder of Algolia, explained to me how diversity was neglected until relatively recently and what the company is doing to change that. "We are fortunate at Algolia that our company culture was designed to be inclusive and has been from the outset, but we did an internal assessment and realized that we were lacking on the diversity side." Historically the company had focused its recruiting efforts on the candidate's skills, interest in the work and the fit with the company's core values. Dessaigne said, "In 2018, we became more proactive about D&I when it dawned on us that we weren't very diverse as a company, especially in the engineering team.

"The D&I drive started organically where a group of people took the initiative to create the ID squad. They swapped the letters around because as a company we believe that if you start with inclusion the diversity will follow. The ID squad launched a bunch of internal and external initiatives, but of course the most impactful one was in recruitment." The company became intentional about its recruitment efforts and decided to proactively source from under-represented minority groups only. Dessaigne continued, "We would still have inbound candidates applying for the various roles, but our outbound sourcing team would only target candidates from diverse backgrounds." It worked. The initiative was started in May and by the end of the year, Algolia had increased the percentage of under-represented minority employees in its engineering team from 4 percent to 11 percent. "We have 200 people in the French office, and I could see the difference when I was there recently, which was great. I am super happy about the outcome. We are continuing to grow our team so our objective for this year is to go from 11 percent to 16 percent within the engineering team. On the one hand building a diverse team becomes easier because diversity attracts diversity. On the other hand, if you are growing as fast as we are you need to hire a lot more people from diverse backgrounds to increase the percentage as much as we want to. D&I is something that we will continue to work on and improve, especially if we want to be able to say we really live our *Care* value."

2. LiveRamp

Anneka Gupta, President of LiveRamp, is the type of person who is never satisfied. "When it comes to Diversity & Inclusion there's always more that we could be doing," she told me. The company has numerous initiatives to promote diversity and inclusion. An example of the work it does in the broader tech community to "redefine the tech-force" and address issues surrounding D&I is the Boundary Breakers series which it highlights at the South by Southwest (SXSW) conference every year.

From a recruiting perspective, the company will focus on the areas where it does not have a diverse enough workforce. "That might be in terms of gender, ethnicity but also age, which for us is a hot topic now because we have a young team and bringing in people with experience is really the most important for us to continue to grow and scale." Gupta continued, "When I, or anybody, sees a team lacking in diversity, we call it out and say, 'We do not have enough perspectives here.' We then talk to those leaders about how we can change it.

"As a company we make it everyone's responsibility to focus on diversity and inclusion and we call it out when we get feedback that we are not living up to our standards." Gupta gave an example of a situation where a leader received feedback from people on his team who did not feel included. "After we discussed the feedback with the team lead he went all in, worked with the people on his team who felt that they weren't being included and figured out what he could change. I'm happy to say that we now have a bunch of women in leadership positions on his team who were not in those positions a year ago, and that the whole outlook of that team and the way they behave has changed. It's important to have company programs and initiatives, which we do, but I think the only way to make D&I work is to make it everyone's responsibility to drive it forward or call it out when there is an issue and work out how to solve it."

3. Periscope Data

Melanie Tantingco, VP of People Operations at Periscope Data, believes that inclusion is foundational because it creates the right environment for diversity to happen. *We are inclusive; We strive to make everyone feel welcome at Periscope Data; We intentionally build diverse teams to create better outcomes for our company and our community* is one of Periscope Data's values, and the company was named among "2018 Best Places to Work" by the *San Francisco Business Times* and has been recognized for building a collaborative, dynamic and inclusive culture. CEO Harry Glaser has been recognized as one of the "Best CEOs for women" and one of the "Best CEOs for diversity" by Comparably.com. "From my perspective a lot of companies get it wrong when they put diversity before inclusion. I believe that if you focus on building an inclusive company then diversity will happen as a result. Inclusion in action is about understanding that you might not have the same opinion as the person across the table from you but you're still operating from a place where you at least want to find common ground or you respect each other enough to agree to disagree. If I have a different opinion to you, I'm not just going to shut down and discount yours. Meeting halfway is just as important." Like Nicolas Dessaigne from Algolia, Tantingco noted that, "A clear advantage of building an inclusive culture and hiring for diversity early on, is that it becomes easier over time. A diverse team naturally attracts diverse candidates because the candidates feel like they can belong."

4. Jellyvision

Jellyvision, unlike a lot of companies, has a Diversity and Inclusion mission statement:

Our purpose at Jellyvision is "Be Helpful"—to people who use our software, to customers who buy it, to our colleagues here at work, and to our communities at large. We've got the best chance to succeed as a truly helpful business, and to be the humans we aspire to be, when Jellyvision's roster includes people of diverse races, backgrounds, genders, sexual orientations, beliefs and abilities. We also need every one of our employees to feel they belong here and that their voice is not just allowed, but respected and sought after.

"I see D&I as a work in progress, not a 'to do,'" said Amanda Lannert, CEO of Jellyvision "It's a muscle that has to get worked, stretched and flexed over time, and we will always have an opportunity to be better and strengthen it. To that end, we have special interest groups, we do unconscious bias training, and we recruit for diversity. We source candidates from under-represented groups and we have created a referral program to encourage people to reach outside their networks and refer talent in." The company publishes diversity statistics every quarter so that people can see what the composition of the company is by leadership level. "Inclusion is much more subjective and therefore much harder to measure, but we try to cover it in the employee engagement survey we run."

The company promotes and maintains diversity and inclusion by:
- Analyzing team and applicant pool demographics quarterly to see where the recruiting process needs adjustment.
- Providing benefits that equitably cover the diversity of their employees.
- Supporting the formation of employee resource inclusion groups to encourage one another to bring their whole selves to work.
- Having everyone on the team, including the CEO, attend interview coaching, unconscious bias training and ongoing education programs.

"When we look at our data we have an excellent representation of gender at all levels of the company; happening to be run by a female CEO helps, I think." One of Lannert's concerns is "about our lack of racial diversity compared to where we draw talent from, and we think a more racially diverse workforce would be better for us, our product and our customers. We are always trying to analyze where any unconscious bias is preventing us from being where we want to be and striving to be a workplace where everyone can grow and thrive."

IN CONCLUSION...

You can't just turn on D&I. It requires management, leadership and a long-term commitment to get right. To some, diversity looks like the easier part of D&I to work on and measure, so leaders tend to confuse a truly D&I-focused culture with merely striving to source diverse candidates for their roles. As we have learned from the companies featured in this chapter, there is much more to it. It makes sense to start by building inclusion (the harder-to-measure subjective part of D&I) into your culture because you will be creating the right environment for diversity to thrive.

Some key takeaways from this chapter:

- Consider setting up an inclusion squad who spearheads internal initiatives and mechanisms to embed the inclusion value.
- Constantly monitor, by means of employee engagement surveys, your team's view on whether you are delivering well on inclusion.
- Arrange unconscious bias training for your team.
- Make it everyone's responsibility to focus on D&I and to call it out when it is not delivered upon.

To attract more diverse employees from a gender, age and cultural diversity perspective, consider the following:

- What do your company's website visuals and copy say and not say about your culture?
- Are your job descriptions written in such a way as to be a deterrent to certain types of candidates?
- Are you severely limiting your candidate pool by sourcing candidates only from "top schools" or specific companies?

- Can you remove telltale signals like the candidate's name, school they went to and where they previously worked from the resume before the evaluation process starts?
- Are you training your interviewers to be aware of different biases—like the "confirmation bias" and "similar to me bias"—that could influence decision-making?

Chapter 12

Remote and Hybrid Work Environments

"You only find out who is swimming naked when the tide goes out."
– Warren Buffet, Chairman & CEO, Berkshire Hathaway

The quote above from the Sage of Omaha is spot on. The pandemic has forced the tide out, and most of the CEOs who ran office-based businesses pre-pandemic are walking around buck naked. These CEOs ignored or put off investing in their culture and unknowingly relied on their office space to hold their undefined and unwritten culture together. The human proximity, camaraderie, "water-cooler moments" (or beer-on-tap moments if they'd drunk the WeWork Kool-Aid) and Friday drinks were enough for them to assume they'd built something resembling a culture. With the pandemic forcing the transition to remote or hybrid work, these "culture isn't critical" type of leaders are finding that what happened naturally because of the office environment will now require a whole new level of application, discipline and commitment.

CHALLENGES AHEAD

Different leadership challenges lie ahead for you and your management team, even if the initial transition to a remote or hybrid work environment has gone smoothly. These challenges were often present in an office environment, but their impact was low enough that they weren't a priority. These could include:

- Coming to terms with the probability that we will not go back to the old "normal" way of doing things.
- Developing new structures, processes and systems to ensure that your team is engaged, connected and motivated.
- Dealing with issues around silo development, team communication and collaboration.
- Ensuring your most productive people don't burn out.
- Dealing with loneliness.
- Looking after your team's mental health.
- Helping the micromanagers in your team come to terms with remote leadership practices.

It is vital that leaders strengthen the glue between their people by developing a new hybrid- or remote-relevant culture for their company. It doesn't matter which route you decide to take, if you don't develop a strong, functional culture your business will suffer. A company like Buffer, which has been a fully remote business since 2015 and is recognized for having a strong culture, still has issues with burnout and still struggles with its remote culture[10]. It follows that you can expect companies that have suddenly been forced to transition to remote or hybrid working to be in for a rude awakening. Depending on the strength of the company's leadership and the culture that's been developed, this awakening could happen as early as the next three months or within the coming twelve. Either way it will happen.

If we understand what was taken for granted pre-pandemic and what is no longer available due to the forced remote/hybrid work situation, we can endeavor to build a remote or hybrid culture that fills those gaps. Some of the in-office experiences that will be missing or be significantly different in a remote or hybrid environment are:

- Proximity – easy to simply lean across your table and have a chat or listen in to a conversation.
- Body language – the ability to "read" how people were feeling.
- Immediacy of communication – we are conditioned to communicate synchronously, and there was an expectation of immediate response.

- Creativity/brainstorming – didn't need a process to brainstorm an idea.
- Informal communication – those "water cooler" moments happened randomly and naturally.
- Information dissemination – for the most part this just happened.
- Feedback – often happened as an informal conversation.
- Recognition and reward – often given publicly or in gatherings.
- Availability and visibility – you could see who was in the office for a quick meeting later that day.
- Control of the environment – you could be specific about the design of your office, the rituals and dress code (even if there was none).
- Structure of the day and week – didn't have to be defined to allow for deep work or informal communication to happen.
- Banter, chat and camaraderie – just happened and a lot of people thrived on it.
- Social events – easy to organize and attend.
- Company culture development – could be delayed or ignored because the impact was not felt immediately.

HYBRID VS. REMOTE

A **hybrid** company has one or more offices at which people can work. Employees may work from the office, remotely, or both.

A **remote** company has no offices, and everyone works from home, or a location of their choosing.

Many leaders think that running a hybrid environment will be easier to do than a fully remote environment. They are wrong. A hybrid environment is actually harder to lead effectively. When everyone is working remotely then "we are all in this together," and everybody shares a similar experience. In a hybrid work environment, you have some people working in an office and others from home, which can create an "us versus them" situation. As a result of this there are a multitude of work challenges that the leaders who decide to run a hybrid work culture have yet to experience. In comparison to the folks in the office, the people working remotely can end up feeling like second-class citizens because they:

- Do not experience work in the same way.
- Do not experience the company culture in the same way.
- Miss out on the banter and other informal communication.
- Do not develop the same relationships.
- Work better asynchronously, whereas their colleagues in the office expect an immediate response to their communication.
- Are often not included in discussions and decisions that take place in the office.
- Are not "visible" to the leadership team (if they are office based).
- Need to be more vocal and fight harder to be heard and recognized.
- Do not always have the same career progression prospects.

The biggest risk for hybrid companies is for their remote employees to feel like they are treated like second-class citizens.

The biggest risk for hybrid companies is for their remote employees to feel like they are treated like second-class citizens. If you don't develop the right processes, structure and disciplines needed by the people who are working remotely, they will eventually leave you. Why would you stay at a company that didn't give you the right tools, processes or structure to fulfill your potential? Remember, there are thousands of remote companies focusing on building a fully remote culture, who will happily recruit your "second-class citizens" if you make the mistake of treating them differently.

I interviewed[11] Andreas Klinger, previously Head of Remote at AngelList and early stage VC at Remote First Capital, and he said, "A 10-person remote team requires the same systems and processes as a 50-person company, and leaders of hybrid teams don't usually understand this." To ensure that the remote people don't feel like second-class citizens, leaders with a hybrid team structure need to, where possible, operate with the discipline and processes of a fully-remote company.

NINE REMOTE WORKING BEST PRACTICES

Leaders who are not experienced in remote working will face many new and ongoing challenges, so it makes sense to try to understand what the best practices around remote work are. The CultureGene Leadership Platform is a software solution that replicates the culture development process I conduct in-person with my clients and is ideal for distributed teams. Over the past eight months, I have been researching remote companies like Gitlab (1,300 employees all remote!), Basecamp, Hotjar, Zapier, Buffer, TopTal, Automattic and others to understand how they operate and to develop the Leadership Platform's software roadmap. From my research I have found that there are nine fundamental best practices that these companies focus on. The nine best practices are:

1. Process-ize the business.
2. Build social connection.
3. Focus on communication.
4. Create and maintain documentation.
5. Add structure.
6. Develop trust and accountability.
7. Focus on output and results.
8. Customize the recruitment and onboarding processes.
9. Become deliberate about culture.

This section discusses seven of the nine best practices. The eighth is covered in Chapters 5 and 6 and the ninth is featured throughout this book.

1. Process-ize Your Business

Company founders often view business processes as rigid and unnecessary enemies to creativity. But when your way of working has been radically altered and the structure that came with working from an office has been lost, solid processes for running meetings properly or onboarding new employees provide the structure and direction your business needs for getting things done. It's not just because your way of working has changed. As Klinger said, "A remote team needs five times more processes in comparison to a co-located team. Take something as simple as a meeting: in a co-located team, you can get a group of people together for a meeting in a matter of minutes, especially when the team is small. Even in a five-person remote team, you need to be better organized and disciplined from the outset." The reason you need to be more organized is that people's individual situations are no longer so similar to each other. Remote workers have more variety, less strict working conditions, less structure, more distractions, less peer pressure and different working hours. All of this places greater stress on traditional assumptions that you made as a leader. Let's look at arranging a meeting as an example. It is one of many invisible processes that happened naturally in an office environment due to people's proximity, visibility and availability, and didn't require a disciplined process. Setting up a meeting is a great example of how remote working reveals the poor management practices of office-based companies. To optimize a meeting in a remote work situation you need to:

1. Decide who should attend.
2. Confirm their availability.
3. Send out meeting invitations.
4. Write up an agenda.
5. Send the pre-read material and agenda to the attendees. The pre-read material and agenda are active documents, so you expect feedback to be given and the discussion to progress before the meeting takes place.
6. Begin and end the meeting on time.
7. Encourage all the attendees to take notes during the meeting.
8. Share the notes, results and deliverables with the attendees as well as members of the team who will be impacted by the decisions made during the meeting.

Not many companies would have had this kind of process in place in an office-based environment, because as Klinger said, "A lot of these things don't happen in co-located teams, either because the team is small enough and they don't need to or because people are lazy and the discipline is not in place."

The clearest way to spot the need for process definition is when there is regular breakdown in communication or where information is being lost between people/teams/departments. At minimum, a newly remote team should start by setting up processes for anything to do with teamwork and communication.

2. Build Social Connection

Fostering a sense of connection without a shared location is one of the most difficult parts of being a remote leader (and for remote working in general). Building social connections between your team members is critical to build a culture of trust within your organization. Leaders should design informal communication into the work week and encourage social time as part of the workday, to make up for what used to happen naturally in the office. You should take an experimental and iterative approach to building and developing social connection. In April 2020 I surveyed[12] 165 startups and found that companies are being creative when it comes to encouraging social connection:

- Morning check-ins (not work-related).
- Book/TV/movie clubs.
- Movie nights using the Netflix party plug in.
- Sharing lunch.
- Holding lunch-and-learn webinars once a week.
- Friday night cocktail parties.
- Fitness class sessions.
- Yoga/group meditation.
- Conference call bingo.
- Team coffees scheduled at specific times throughout the day.
- Collaborative quizzes on Kahoot.
- Green – Yellow – Red personal status updates, where each team member holds up a colored prop and then explains how they feel and why.
- Shared Google doc for company and personal news.
- Weekly scheduled "water-cooler" calls, during which people chat about whatever they like.
- "What I did over the weekend" email thread.
- Pizza all-hands meetings with the pizza and delivery paid for.
- Dress up/hat themes for daily all-hands calls.

- Group training and one-to-one learning sessions.
- Voice note updates via Otter.ai.

3. Focus on Communication

In an office setting, the natural instinct is to have an in-person conversation with someone. There are many ways to interact with a colleague: team meetings, brainstorming, asking a quick question across the room, over lunch, catching up in the break room, or just listening to what people are saying around you. These in-person luxuries are no longer automatically available in a remote or hybrid work setting, and leaders of remote companies work hard to ensure that communication is flowing in their organizations. Leaders need to set a cadence for regular communication and think about how they use the different communication channels available to them:

- Synchronous communication, as the name implies, is where a group of people use the same method of communication, and hence is synchronized (e.g., phone calls, video conference calls or meetings). Response is immediate, there and then.
- Asynchronous communication is a back-and-forth exchange in writing (some teams use video clips) that happens as and when people can respond (e.g. email, workflow management platforms and messaging apps).
- Informal communication is non-work related and enables groups of people with similar interests to form. There are two types of informal communication: both kinds need to be preserved in a remote environment, but they need different approaches, and what is needed for one can be heavy-handed for the other:
    – Convenient informal communication happens whether the company does anything about it or not. Groups of parents, people who have dogs as pets or employees bad-mouthing the leadership can form naturally. It helps strengthen the culture if the leadership team promotes the formation of the "positive" groups of people with common interests.
    – Circumstantial informal communication is designed

into the working week of the company by the leadership team, creating opportunities where informal communication can happen.

Remote work can be that much more productive and enjoyable if you get communication right. Andreas Klinger noted, "A well-structured remote work setup typically leads to fewer distractions and office politics, a quieter noise level and fewer, more efficient meetings. Done properly, online communication tools allow for greater transparency between departments, which avoids teams getting siloed and opens conversations up to the wider company." In an age of mass digital distraction, abysmally low levels of employee engagement and the unprecedented levels of change and uncertainty, these benefits have transformational potential.

4. Create and Maintain Documentation

Your people will need as much visibility into their colleagues' work as they would have previously had in an office, where they could easily meetup, listen in, chat over lunch, have a beer, etc. The only way for this to happen in a remote work environment (in the absence of a companywide pro-active, "in-advance" communication capability, which most companies do not have) is if people document pretty much everything.

I discussed the importance of processes earlier in this chapter, and documentation is the most effective way of communicating those processes to the company. Documentation is crucial for new joiners to get up to speed on the culture and relevant projects they will be working on. Current team members have a knowledge base to revert to when joining a new project or catching up on different initiatives that they have not been working on directly.

Remote companies like Gitlab take a handbook-first approach to documentation, creating a single source of truth[13] for the company to operate from. As the Gitlab handbook explains, "A handbook-first approach to documentation is sneakily vital to a well-run business. While it feels skippable, inefficient even, the outsized benefits of intentionally writing down and organizing process, culture and solutions are staggering." Information silos, which can form naturally in office-based environments, are far more destructive in remote companies where the combination of asynchronous communication and knowledge gaps can leave team members unable to do their jobs properly and can degrade trust. Human beings expect to operate in synchronicity, and those people who are used to working in an office struggle to transition from a "speak first" to a "write first" mentality. Getting documentation right is crucial to ensuring that silos are avoided, any knowledge loss is minimized and communication happens smoothly across your team.

5. Add Structure

If you previously were office-based, your people experienced your company culture face-to-face and in an environment that you could, for the most part, control. With your team working remotely they are now experiencing your culture digitally at their home, which is an environment and culture of its own, that you have limited control over. One thing that you need to think about with an office-based team is your culture is now competing with your employee's home culture. It's also essential to remember that the structure of your people's workday has changed dramatically. The office gave an artificial structure to your team's workday that has been lost, and leaders shouldn't expect their people to understand how to be as effective at home as they were in the office. For most people, working from home doesn't involve a 9 o'clock start and 5 o'clock (or later) finish, as it may have been the case in the office. Most people need structure, and a lack of it could impact efficiency and productivity dramatically.

According to David Darmanin, cofounder and CEO of Hotjar, "A structured work week is crucial for the efficient running of a remote shop." The company's weekly structure is described in their online Team Manual[14]:

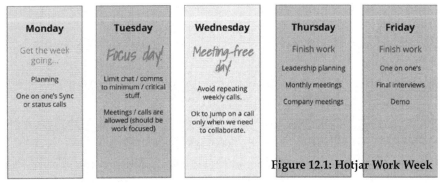

Figure 12.1: Hotjar Work Week

Mondays: Call-heavy days! We have our planning meetings, 1-1s, sync calls, etc., on Monday. People are likely to be in meetings for the large part of the day, so they might be a bit slower when it comes to responding to messages.

Tuesdays: Focus days! Tuesdays are generally the most productive working days of the week. Having a focus day on Tuesday allows each team member to focus more on their sprints. We try to avoid having regularly scheduled meetings on Tuesdays unless they are project-centric. This doesn't mean that communication or cross-team collaboration is off the table—we can't work without speaking to each other, neither do we want to encourage this! Other team members are less likely to be tied up in meetings on Tuesdays.

Wednesdays: No meeting Wednesdays! We never schedule calls on Wednesdays unless it is an emergency. People will jump on quick calls as necessary to collaborate, and still communicate via Slack/email.

Thursdays + Fridays: All our "big" meetings are scheduled for these days—weekly demos, monthly meetings, Leadership planning, etc. How call-busy people are will depend on the week we are in during the month.

Leaders have to figure out where structure is required and where there can be flexibility. To maximize team collaboration Hotjar suggests that team members overlap their "online availability" time, as much as possible. "Online availability refers to your 'online' time on Slack and 'availability' for calls with colleagues on Hangouts. For this reason, we require as a minimum you are 'available' every day between 2pm–5pm CET."

The Hotjar structure is one alternative. There are people who would feel that this could be a somewhat oppressive and suffocating environment. It's up to you as a leader to evaluate what amount of structure is needed for your business.

6. Develop Trust and Accountability

Trust is a critical component for any successful business, but it is critical for remote working. The tried and tested method of developing trust in successful remote companies is through being as transparent as possible. Most successful remote companies are built on a foundation of transparency, trust and accountability.

If trust and accountability are missing, leaders believe they need to micromanage.

If trust and accountability are missing, leaders believe they need to micromanage. Their employees end up either:

1. Doing the bare minimum: they "work-to-rule" and choose to spend time in politics rather than execution, overall; they focus on "cover-my-ass."

2. Feeling that they need to prove themselves by overworking. Overworking leads to lower individual productivity, lower reliability and creates lower team productivity, which could lead to increased stress and ultimately, burnout.

Muriel Maignan Wilkins writing for the Harvard Review[15] has this to say on micromanagement:

"While micromanaging may get you short-term results, over time it negatively impacts your team, your organization, and yourself. You dilute your own productivity and you run out of capacity to get important things done. You stunt your team members' development and demoralize them. You create an organizational vulnerability when your team isn't used to functioning without your presence and heavy involvement."

Leaders of successful remote companies build trust by focusing on clearly defined goals, alignment of ownership and responsibility, and accountability of output. There is good reason for this: another Harvard study[16], (looking at trust in professional teams) found that high-trust teams report:

- 74% less stress.
- 106% more energy at work.
- 50% higher productivity.
- 13% fewer sick days.

- 76% more engagement.
- 29% more satisfaction with their lives.
- 40% less burnout.

Tamara Littleton is the founder and CEO of The Social Element (formerly Emoderation), an award-winning social media management agency based in London practicing a hybrid work strategy. Littleton believes that it is possible to build a fully remote culture, but it's also hard to do, because crucial aspects of the relationship—the ability to read and feed off each other's body language, to eat with people—are lost. Littleton continued, "I think that encouraging and creating an environment where people can share food and drink together is key to building a strong culture. Those in-person experiences allow different conversations to happen, and it's harder to facilitate that in a fully remote environment. Even simple chitchatting can create bonds. You learn things about people you wouldn't have known otherwise."

Despite feeling that some things are lost when people work remotely, Littleton is realistic that not all workers need to be in an office setting and is a firm believer that a critical aspect of running a hybrid work company is trust. High levels of trust are needed because, "As a leader you must assume that people are going to get on with it and do the right thing. We treat people well, and we're highly communicative with and trusting of them. I think that has given us the edge in running a hybrid company. Another aspect to consider is without trust, remote teams lose a vast amount of time in waiting and checking/double-checking. Because round-trip communications are slower in remote working, any "wait" is massively magnified."

It is worth taking a moment to let that sink in. You build trust in a remote environment by focusing on output (what gets done) rather than input (when, where and how many hours a person worked).

When it comes to remote work it's not about the hours worked, it's all about the output.

7. Focus on Output and Results
When it comes to remote work it's not about the hours worked, it's all

about the output. Leaders who could see their team working in the office struggle to move away from the idea of hours worked as a reliable indicator of the impact delivered. On the other hand, leaders in successful remote teams understand that they need to trust their teams to get on with it and focus on output, impact and results instead. Leaders of remote teams must be able to hold their teams accountable. To do this they need to combine clarity about the deliverables of the task or project with:

- Measuring output against timelines.
- Monitoring through check-ins and one-to-ones.
- Evaluating the impact and results of the work.
- Assessing employee output and holding team members accountable.

Consider that not all employees have the same competencies or levels of experience. Junior employees who, in an office environment, would have had access to more experienced executives to shadow, ask questions and learn from, will now require more mentoring and monitoring to achieve the desired output in a remote environment.

Dame Stephanie "Steve" Shirley CH DBE FREng FBCS is an entrepreneur turned ardent philanthropist. An IT tech pioneer, she started Freelance Programmers, a remote work company, in 1962 with a capital of just £6 and built it into a software development powerhouse. Dame Stephanie was the first female CEO of a high-growth software development company.

The business was founded at a time when software was given away free as part of the IT hardware sale, but Dame Stephanie could see where the value of the IT sale was heading. "There had never been a company like us before and Harvard Business Review wrote about us as 'the company without offices,' because remote working was unheard of at the time." The company was started to provide jobs for women with children and of the first 300 staff, 297 were female. "Many of Britain's best programmers were females who couldn't get back into the male-dominated workforce because they had left jobs when they got married or fell pregnant." These brilliant minds were stuck at home with time and brain power to spare and Dame Stephanie's "company without offices" was the perfect opportunity for them to work flexibly.

At the time, in traditional companies, people had to clock in and clock out using punch cards and had their pay docked if they spent too much time at lunch. Freelance Programmers was different. "We paid our people for the work they completed, it didn't matter how, as long as it was well done," she explained to me. The freelancers the company employed were trusted to make the best use of their time to complete the projects they were working on. This is a valuable lesson, as relevant then, as it is today.

The output and results focused approach worked well for Freelance Programmers. The company floated on the London Stock Exchange in 1996, and at its peak in 2000, Freelance Programmers, or FI, as it was re-branded, had a market capitalization of $1.5 billion, employed 6,000 people and generated a turnover of $550 million. Remarkably, Dame Stephanie was never in it for money; she merely wanted to create a work environment where there was no prejudice or preconceived notions about what a woman could or couldn't do. Dame Stephanie has over the years gifted or donated most of her wealth—more than $80 million—to her staff and charity through the Shirley Foundation.

IN CONCLUSION...

Culture is the glue that keeps your team together and in most companies that glue will be stretched and stressed in the coming months. It is your responsibility as a leader, whether you decide to go fully remote or build a hybrid work environment, to understand how the pandemic has changed and is changing your company's culture. Work out what elements of your culture worked and are still relevant. Consider the way you work now and will need to work in the future. Depending on which operating model you choose, start to define and embed the new culture you will need to execute a successful remote or hybrid work culture.

Whether your company plans to go fully remote or hybrid, the strength of your culture will largely determine whether your business will overcome the challenges and take advantage of the opportunities that will arise.

Focus on developing your capability in the seven best practices mentioned in this chapter.

1. Start to process-ize your business by asking your team to analyze the differences and complexities of how they used to

work, compared to how they work now. If the way they work now is significantly more complex, then you should consider developing and documenting it as a disciplined process.

2. Be deliberate about social connection and build informal communication into the structure of the week.

3. Develop good communication habits and define which channels should be used for the different types of communication.

4. Document everything that happens that is important to the way the company operates to enable a stronger, more informed, more trusting, and more connected team.

5. Block off time for deep focused work, meetings, calls, etc. for you and your team to give them the structure they need.

6. Be clear about what outputs you require and trust the team to manage their time, days and responsibilities around that agreed output.

7. Be as transparent as possible as it improves credibility, lowers the chances of miscommunication and builds trust.

Chapter 13

Multiple Office Environments

"Culture makes people understand each other better."
– Paulo Coelho, Brazilian lyricist and novelist

With multiple office locations, you must think about how you are going to embed the relevant parts of your company culture into the local culture of the different offices. Having multiple offices, as well as offices in multiple countries, will change the dynamics of your culture, but it does not mean that the original values and culture need to be thrown out. The values are the business's core DNA and should remain the same. "The way we do things around here" can be adapted to work across the different offices.

Two of the most prominent difficulties companies face when they have more than one office include:

1. Ensuring that the company's values are integrated into and lived across the different offices.
2. Ensuring that the leadership team understands which subcultures are forming across the various offices and what they need to do to stop information and communication silos from happening.

Subcultures develop naturally. They develop around functional units (engineering team vs. sales team), shared educational backgrounds, past company experience, geographic location, the dominant occupation in an office, even smoking or going for a drink after work—anything that people have in common.

Getting cross-functional teams to work well together is not easy, mainly because each team brings their business goals and functional jargon to the project, which more often than not results in issues around communication, reaching agreement and (if you get that far) implementation. Apart from the different goals and priorities, each team can also often have different meanings they use. Think for a moment about how differently an AI engineer, customer services rep or sales manager could potentially interpret the word "marketing."

The solution is for leaders to create opportunities for the teams to get to know one another, share information and knowledge learn, and to communicate effectively by understanding one another's drivers, communication styles and subcultures.

By looking at both the micro and macro elements of a new office's culture, a company can achieve coherent values and culture across multiple locations. There are elements like language or national culture that might seem impossible to overcome, but if looked at correctly a company can integrate and adapt to maintain a cohesive company culture across offices, borders and even languages.

In this chapter I look at how Emarsys makes adaptations to the delivery of its values for different countries. Thread focuses on hiring a leader for its warehouse operations who lives the values and knows how to hire for those values. Guidion realizes that it doesn't make sense for employees in its new German office to speak English as a first language in the office. Algolia, on the other hand, decided early on that it is a global company, and as such, everyone who works there should speak English in the office. The Ballou CEO believes it is vital to carry the company values from office to office herself, tailoring her visits to major events or critical times for each of the three teams. Influitive rotates the responsibility of leading the Daily Sync-Up Meeting among the various offices to ensure that each office leads the meeting and feels like it is the headquarters for the day. I will also explore how CloudMade overcomes a culture communication false start.

1. Emarsys

Emarsys CEO Ohad Hecht takes a subtle approach to ensuring his company's culture is being lived across the 16 countries in which they have offices. "When you look at different countries you must respect the local and national culture. America is very different, for instance, from Germany, whether we like it or not. Sometimes in America the communication can be very positive and upbeat, and while that communication is perceived as normal in the US, in Budapest and Germany and much of Europe it is seen as being "happy clappy."

At Emarsys, there is some adaptation, not to the core values, but to the delivery of the values throughout the company. The outcome of this is that offices in different countries have come up with similar but different ways to promote the living of the values, based on what's important to the people in that office.

Hecht explained, "In Austria, the delivery of the *We are one* value is around volunteering to help homeless people. In Germany, people help at animal shelters. In the US, it's about packing meals for hungry children. With a company spread across 16 offices you have to allow for some local nuance to the delivery of the values, otherwise the values are not organic or authentic." How the local teams deliver on them is entirely up to them as long as they respect the company's core values.

2. Thread

Thread founder Kieran O'Neill and his team know firsthand that the consistent enactment of culture doesn't just happen spontaneously or haphazardly. Before the company separated its headquarters from its warehouse, the issue of tending to multiple locations didn't exist. Every team member was used to attending lunch together, regrouping at meetings and interacting with everybody else on a daily basis. When the team split to two sites, O'Neill realized that the company needed to quickly figure out how to recreate that shared culture before the values dissolved and the team fell apart.

"Having a strong, values-oriented culture in one location doesn't mean you will automatically get the same in the second location," O'Neill warned. "Many people in the warehouse see the job as a great way of earning extra income, but don't see Thread as their long-term career plan, which is totally fine. The tricky part for us was to get a match—or at the very least buy-in—to the values when somebody wasn't going to be here for the long haul."

The solution to this was hiring the right people. O'Neill's first step to achieving this was to recruit a manager for the new warehouse who was a great values match for the business. Someone who was able to demonstrate that they lived the values naturally and had a track record of hiring effectively for those values. As O'Neill reiterated to me, "Transferring the culture to multiple locations is first and foremost about ensuring that the leader for that location has a strong fit with the values, vision and mission of the company, so that they in turn can recruit the right people below them."

As I discussed in Chapter 5, if you have defined your values and the expected behaviors that are associated with those values you can build a database of values-based interview questions. Those interview questions can be customized for the role and seniority level you are hiring for. In this way you can create specific questions to interview for a warehouse manager and then do the same for part-time or short-term staff.

3. Guidion

When Amsterdam-based Guidion opened a new branch in Germany, Maarten Roerink's approach was to allow the team to build its own subculture. This subculture would be relevant to the people in the office, considering the social, ethnic and geographical differences that needed to be considered. As Roerink explained, "In the Netherlands, for example, everybody speaks English as a first or second language; therefore, the meetings can be held in English. In Germany, that's not the case, so the meetings are held in German."

Subcultures will and should develop naturally around the functional units of the company and depend on the cultural context of the location as well as on the specific employees who are involved there. Yet the subculture must always remain a part of a greater whole: the overarching umbrella culture, consisting of the company's non-negotiable core values and vision. It is this exact overarching culture that Roerink described as "the unique way of working within Guidion that's created our success." He said that the company's core values "remain at the center of who we are, and we will ensure that they are the same and incorporated into the processes of the German business and any other country we expand to." To ensure a deep understanding of the core values and an easy transfer of the culture, Roerink and his team focused on hiring people whose values aligned with Guidion's. They spent time in Germany with the team and invested in training the team on the values and what it means to live the Guidion culture.

4. Ballou

Colette Ballou may be based in London, but she operates across all three of Ballou's offices. "I travel a lot," she said. "I have three excellent GMs who I trust deeply, and they are empowered to run their offices. They have full control over their P&Ls. And they know when to bring me in to help solve things." Although she has hired great people and given them "freedom to be awesome," Ballou still knows that it is her responsibility as a leader to spend time in each office and, crucially, show up when needed. This is particularly critical when dealing with the larger chessboard of multiple locations. "I spend time in the offices every month and also will visit when I feel that it is important for me to be in a certain office at a certain time," she explained.

"A good example of this was before the Brexit vote, where I planned to be with the UK team on that day of the result. I didn't expect Brexit to happen, of course, but I'm glad I hedged my bets and was with the team that day. I was able to soothe jittery nerves by speaking to the team about what Brexit might mean for us and how we would adapt where necessary. We expected some currency fluctuations, and a weaker pound could be beneficial for the business. I made sure everyone understood that we had a plan and that there were no jobs on the line and no offices would have to close. Essentially that there was no immediate threat and there might actually be opportunities for us."

Ballou didn't leave her other teams in the dark. She practiced transparency and confidence as she penned and sent a thorough company-wide email summarizing the UK team meeting, also sharing what Brexit meant for the company and what Ballou's strategy would be going forward.

5. Influitive

Influitive's Daily Sync-Up Meeting, which I discussed in Chapter 8, runs for nine minutes, is mandatory for all employees, and is open to anyone else who wishes to join from their network. This meeting brings together all of Influitive's employees, including the ones who work in other offices. It is usually led out of the company's home base of Toronto. One day a week, however, Mark Organ, Executive Chairman, has ensured that the meeting is hosted from the Boston or London office, "so that the HQ team understands what it feels like to be remote." As Organ puts it, the daily all-hands meeting is the "heartbeat of the business" and it's important that the other offices take responsibility for running it.

6. Algolia

Nicolas Dessaigne, cofounder of Algolia, understands the need to be flexible with cultural rules and to be considerate of time zone challenges when expanding internationally. "I think it's very important to try to create one culture for one company. I don't think of our company as French, British or American. We are global." To reinforce the global approach, the founders introduced a rule early on that everybody speaks English at Algolia.

At the same time, Dessaigne understands that you can't be too rigid in how you apply rules about culture. "We just opened a new office in Tokyo where the culture is different, and the market is different. I know that for the first handful of people we hire in Tokyo, English will be okay. But if we continue to insist on English-speaking employees only, we won't have the best chance for success. There's no way we can hire only English speakers if we want to scale that office to 20 or 50 people."

Expanding east when you have a strong presence in Europe and the US also has its time zone challenges. "We have our all-hands meeting every Tuesday at 8:30 a.m. in San Francisco, which is 5:30 p.m. in Paris. In Tokyo that's the middle of the night. Today we have one person in Tokyo who can watch the recording of it, so it's not a problem, but that's not going to work for a larger team. As with all our culture challenges we will find a way." Dessaigne understands that Algolia will have to do things differently in Tokyo.

7. CloudMade

Nick Black is the President and cofounder of CloudMade, a London headquartered company that designs and develops personalization software for cars. The company has scaled from a team of 35 twenty-four months ago to 120 people, 90 of which are based in Ukraine. When we spoke about leading decentralized teams Black explained how, to overcome a false start with communicating the culture to the team, CloudMade had to run a two-day culture development off-site meeting to get everyone on the same page. "We made the classic mistake when launching our mission, vision and values of not considering the traditional Ukrainian culture and that resulted in us not getting our message across."

How did this happen? The founders had defined the mission and vision statements and worked with the rest of the leadership team to define the company values. During the presentation to the team they decided to make the seven values more relevant to the audience by having Values Ambassadors present them. "We asked people who we thought exemplified a value to be the Values Ambassadors. Each ambassador explained which of the seven values they were representing and talked about how they embodied that value in the way they behaved in the business." This could have worked, but for a simple mistake, as Black explained. "The key issue was that most of our ambassadors were not Ukrainian, which is where most of our team is. Instead of people from our London office we should have chosen more people from the Kyiv team to be our ambassadors."

The lack of understanding and acceptance became apparent after the presentation. American English is the standard language used to do business at CloudMade, but for most people in Kyiv it's not their first language and it's not compulsory to speak English internally. "Even though we had defined the values and the expected behaviors associated with those values, our people still couldn't interpret what the values meant; the phrasing wasn't understood. For example, no one really understood what *grit* meant," Black told me. "There is no direct translation of grit to Ukrainian. Did we want them to be like the stuff you put on the road? This led to a ton of confusion. Similarly, one of our values *go big or go home*—a classic mantra in Silicon Valley—translated really badly. The team found it overly aggressive—like we were telling people to quit before they had even gotten started."

"We got a lot of feedback that people didn't understand the values, mission or the vision," Black said, and that feedback was the genesis for the two-day off-site meeting. Black told me that he wanted to invest the time to do it properly this time. "We went through a process where a subset of the team became the values team. They surveyed their colleagues to see what they felt of the values and they re-wrote the values in English and Ukrainian. They then worked with a copywriter to translate the values from Ukrainian (the mother tongue of 90% of our staff) back to English. We did this to make sure that linguistically we had phrasing that worked in Ukrainian and English / Anglo cultures."

Ukraine is well known for the outsourcing of software development. Engineers are typically used to being told what to do and then doing it and this is part of the culture that Black and his team were, and are, trying to change. "Success," in Black's words, "is for our team not to expect to be told what to do, success is gaining an understanding of the problem, figuring out what needs to be done and then doing it at the office." Black and the team set out to help people to understand that they could and should take ownership and be leaders.

As well as stretching his team, the off-site meeting helped Black himself to develop new skills. "I've never led a team of 120 people before," he said, "and something I'm learning is the huge value of having people make their own mistakes. It's important to create an environment where people feel they are able to make mistakes, own up to, and learn from them."

The off-site meeting was a success and started CloudMade on the process of changing the culture of the team in Ukraine. "There is lot of work still to be done, but the meaning of our values, mission and vision is clear, and our people understand what being responsible and taking ownership mean."

IN CONCLUSION...

Successfully maintaining your company's culture and values across multiple offices requires a multifaceted approach. If you have employees who are based in another city or country, if they speak a different home language, if they work remotely or from an office, you need to consider the cultural dynamics of their working and living environment. Certain elements of "the way you work" may not transfer across to their local culture and you may need to be flexible with how you operate. You can be flexible on how your values are delivered but you should not compromise on your core (non-negotiable) values and what they mean to the company.

The action points explored in this chapter include:

1. Try to understand your various office locations' local culture so that you can determine how flexible you need to be with your "culture rules."
2. Translate and communicate your vision, mission and values into the local country language to ensure there is no misinterpretation.
3. Focus on developing communication processes that make it easier for those outside the headquarters to participate and feel like they're a part of the team.
4. Recognize when subcultures form and embrace it as long as the subculture members are using the company's values as the non-negotiable foundation for how it operates.
5. Consider allowing for adaptations to how the values are delivered, so that offices in different cities or countries can come up with their own authentic ways to promote how they live the company values.
6. Recruit a leader who you know is a good fit with the values or send a "culture ambassador" to lead or work in the new location.
7. Rotate the hosting and running of daily or weekly global meetings among the satellite offices to share responsibility and give everyone an understanding what it feels like to be remote.

Chapter 14

Conclusion

Culture happens whether you like it or not. It initially develops as a random collection of good and bad behaviors, norms, habits, beliefs, rituals, communication styles, processes and policies, which can be crafted into an asset for the business or ignored to become a potential liability. To the culture-driven leader culture is not a tick-box exercise, nor a vague, loosely held-together set of ideas that might or might not be shared by the company; culture is a critical business function that must be defined, embedded and managed daily.

Culture is a complex function because it happens below the surface; it is, for the most part, invisible, subconscious and intangible. The culture-driven leader uses vision and mission statements, combined with a set of well-defined values (and expected behaviors) to bring the culture to the surface and make it real and liveable for all employees of the company. The vision, mission, and values provide guidelines and structure to the team and new joiners about why the company exists, what they can expect from the company, what they need to do to succeed at the company and how they need to do it.

What I've set out to do with *Own Your Culture* is to share a set of discussions on culture that tell a story about what culture is, why it matters, how to embed it in your company and how to manage it. If your company doesn't currently have a strong, functional culture, then you have seen in this book that you have a myriad of opportunities to work on. You can change your current behavior model and begin defining and building what will eventually become understood by the team as your actual culture. I say behavior model, because culture isn't just a way of thinking, but a way of acting—something we can recognize, reward, measure, train for and change if you put the effort in.

Your culture is impervious to the competition; they can't copy your culture, nor can they interfere with it. The health and strength of the culture you build is up to you. A surefire way to start to poison your culture is to hire people who don't match your values. This is the reason why it's vital to incorporate your values and expected behaviors into the hiring process and the other processes of your company. Another way to start to poison your culture is for you or your management team to behave in ways that do not match your espoused values. Incorporating them into the functions of your business ensures that your leadership team, who will each have their own style and capabilities, strengths and weaknesses, are aligned and understand how to live the culture. If nurtured and managed properly, your company culture is the one sustainable competitive advantage that you have complete control over. You can start to take control by taking the examples in this book and testing them in your company.

Bretton Putter
July 2020

P.S. WANT TO CHANGE THE WORLD?

The CultureGene **Vision** is to improve the working lives of millions of people by changing the culture of business globally.

The CultureGene **Mission** is to define the culture development process as a critical business function in the same way that finance, sales, marketing and engineering are.

To achieve our vision and mission we are building a software-based Culture Leadership Platform to assist current and future generations of leaders in building strong, functional cultures for their companies.

You can reach us at brett@culturegene.ai if you are interested in finding out more about the CultureGene software and consultancy services, joining our team, partnering with us, or if you simply want to help us make the world a better place.

BONUS: If you want to get your hands on a copy of my first book *Culture Decks Decoded* you can download the free PDF version at https://www.culturegene.ai/books/culture-decks-decoded

Afterword

From Culture-Driven to Deliberately Developmental Leadership

Congratulations if you've gotten this far in the book. I hope that *Own Your Culture* has given you the tools and a clear pathway toward becoming a culture-driven leader and developing and maintaining a strong, functional company culture. Company culture is always evolving and so should culture leadership. This afterword explores what the future of culture leadership could look like.

Own Your Culture focuses on the many applicable ways in which the leadership of a company can create and maintain a strong, functional culture. However, in their book, *An Everyone Culture*, Robert Kegan and Lisa Lahey Laskow go one step further, describing an approach to leadership that has the power and potential to impact the people who work in companies like never before. They describe Deliberately Developmental Leadership (DDL), which, I believe, is the next evolution of the culture-driven leader.

Deliberately Developmental Leadership is a derivative of Deliberately Developmental Organizations (DDOs)—a term coined by Kegan and Laskow—which refers less to a style of leadership and more to an entire philosophy and approach to leadership that goes beyond traditional business leadership as we know it today. They profiled three extraordinary companies in their book—Bridgewater

Associates, Next Jump and Decurion—and have thought deeply about workplace culture and the role that the personal growth of their people plays in their culture. These companies have taken it so far that the entire functioning of the business has meaningful personal development in its every fiber. Everything revolves around the simple but profound idea that when a business pursues and prioritizes profitability *alongside* continuous and explicit focus of developing its people, everyone wins. In a DDO absolutely everyone—from the most senior people to the newest hires—is deeply engaged in an ongoing, relentless and intense personal growth journey, which is in part achieved by focusing on exploring and understanding a person's weaknesses—their impediments to success—rather than their strengths. Everything, from meetings to working practices, from the way people are hired, onboarded and evaluated, all the way through to how they are let go. From the way the businesses' purpose is understood, to how it translates and comes to life in the organizations, coaching, high potential programs and the like are not reserved for the few. They are for everyone and they are designed into the Operating System of the company. That is why these companies create what Kegan and Laskow call an "everyone culture." Adopting a DDL mentality makes leadership more productive, more fulfilling, and incredibly rewarding, as you see the people around you come to terms with their weaknesses... and flourish.

Here are six fundamental principles to bear in mind if transitioning from a culture-driven leader to a DDL appeals to you.

1. Rethink Happiness

Happiness can be thought of, as Kegan and Laskow point out, as a state fundamentally characterized by pleasure. Typically, in our society, we attempt to achieve this through banishing pain and boredom. The other way we tend to try to reach this state of pleasure is through pursuing the experience of positive emotions—and there is almost no limit as to how people do this.

But there is a second definition of happiness (which overlaps with the first but is distinct in some ways): happiness occurs within a process of human flourishing. Inherent in this perspective is the understanding that difficulty, struggles, and even emotional and psychological pain and stress are not things to be avoided; if experienced in the pursuit of growth, challenges and pain can ultimately contribute to a sense of deep meaning and fulfillment. This, in turn, engenders happiness.

Although it is less appealing in some ways—because it involves embracing rather than avoiding discomfort—we can all relate to this second definition of happiness. Perhaps you remember a project that kept you working late into the night, night after night, but which ultimately became one of the proudest accomplishments in your life. Maybe you recall a sense of being "in over your head" when launching a new project and the sense of satisfaction that arose when you delivered it. Perhaps you have spent many hours trying to master a complex skill such as learning an instrument, and you can remember the frustration of repeatedly getting it wrong, but also the great feelings that come with small breakthroughs.

Anyone pursuing a creative endeavor knows that frustration is an inherent and utterly necessary part of the process. Whatever your personal experience, understanding how critical the distinction is between the concept of happiness that aims to banish pain and suffering versus realizing that in the pursuit of flourishing, struggling can hold enormous value. Athletes know this. Entrepreneurs know it. Actors developing a character with richness and depth know it. "Pressure creates diamonds and fire refines gold. "As clichéd as this can sound, it is also a powerful and often accurate metaphor.

2. Grow as a Leader Under Pressure

It is a common experience for people in leadership positions to be the target of overt and covert psychological pressure from those they lead, to somehow make work less stressful and challenging. Leaders are often subconsciously asked to contain the pressure their direct reports feel and to not show any stress so that those around them do not feel it either. In the metaphor commonly used in the hospitality industry, leaders are asked to be like swans: visibly graceful, with all effort and franticness hidden away from others' view. At the same time, enormous pressure can land on leaders from those more senior to them in a system. The pressure to deliver, to meet deadlines, and to get it right can be very stressful and challenging to manage.

It is therefore essential for a leader to hold onto the knowledge that difficulty, stress, and even being somewhat overwhelmed can be helpful, provided you know how to handle it and what to do with it. It can also be a useful reminder for leaders who might feel compelled to remove all stress and difficulty for their direct reports, or those who find it hard to watch other people struggle.

3. Pursue Achievement At all Costs?

Type A personalities have always done well in our wider culture. They are the high-flying executives that sometimes have a reputation for being willing to achieve at any cost to themselves and those around them, resulting in burnout and countless broken relationships. Type A leaders are sometimes susceptible to demanding of their reports the same sacrifices; pursuing goal attainment and achievement at all costs. Think about the characters from the TV series *Suits*: as the seasons progress, the show depicts many main characters who have achieved great successes at enormous personal cost. Is this personal sacrifice really necessary? DDOs show us that pursuing excellence does not have to happen at the cost to people's well-being and fulfillment.

Framing "achievement" as something to be pursued alongside and in parallel to one's growth can help the most driven of leaders keep an eye on the bigger picture and to think about the values and hidden desires underpinning what they are pursuing. Think about whether and how your direct reports' efforts toward executing on key business goals are taking place in the pursuit of their personal growth.

4. Make Weaknesses Public

We all carry a mental image of a leader publicly shaming their direct reports for their failings and weaknesses. No wonder most of us spend a lot of time "hiding, lying and faking" in the workplace, to use a phrase that is part of the everyday parlance at the DDO Next Jump. The amount of energy, time and creativity that is poured into covering up weaknesses is a travesty.

To make your and your employees weaknesses public might be easy to misinterpret. It is not about shaming or humiliating anyone.

In fact, to do this well, you need to be willing to learn to be transparent about your own weaknesses first and foremost.

The thinking behind this suggestion comes from how DDOs conceptualize weaknesses and failure. It is an obvious yet vital observation that most of us invest a considerable amount of energy into hiding our weak points, playing a strategic game of hide-and-seek in the office. This does not serve anyone well: it keeps our weak points fenced off, cut off from feedback and space to grow; it sends a silent message to those we work with that having room left to grow is unacceptable (reminiscent of a fixed rather than a growth mindset). This, in turn, reinforces the message that they should also hide, lie and fake their way through the day; and it costs us, our teams and the organizations we work for a lot of time and energy.

An alternative approach, and one that is already at work in some organizations, involves naming and explicitly discussing your weaknesses and failings, bringing out into the open what most of us would instinctively want to hide. This is challenging and needs to be done on a foundation of trust and within a suitable framework. One that starts by understanding that people's flaws or development areas are being spoken about not to shame, minimize or hold power over anyone, but to further their growth and development. Work by Carol Dweck, author and Professor of Psychology at Stanford, on "fixed" and "growth" mindsets highlights that at a certain point in childhood, children begin to reject learning. The realization that they have not achieved mastery becomes painful as the child develops self-consciousness. Unless and until a person can face and take ownership of their flaws they cannot grow.

While it may seem counterintuitive, the more people engage in these kinds of practices—naming and taking ownership of their weak points, usually through a process of self-reflection and receiving far more honest feedback than most of us are used to hearing—the more they report enjoying it. The psychological discomfort of hearing about what you don't do well is rarely comfortable, but over time it becomes manageable and can indicate to you that you are growing. Even hearing the same feedback over and over again, which people at Next Jump sometimes report, can prove to be invaluable and can reveal to you that you are open, curious, willing and maybe even brave. I believe it takes guts to face our flaws. It is easier to focus purely on external factors, and in business there are ample opportunities to do so.

A Deliberately Developmental Leader understands the power of self-awareness as the ultimate business secret weapon (if there is such a thing). How you facilitate and foster that will very much depend on the kind of organization or team you run. You might initiate a check in at the start and/or end of every team meeting, like at Decurion Corporation, one of the companies featured in *An Everyone Culture*. You might foster psychological safety through the practice of vulnerable leadership. You might integrate exercises such as "The Shadow You Cast" on team away days.

Making weaknesses public—others' and your own—brings the personal firmly into the realm of the professional. It requires a level of emotional intelligence and maturity that in decades gone by would have seemed completely out of place to all but the seemingly most radical of thinkers. Yet with work such as Brené Brown's *Dare to Lead: Brave Work. Tough Conversations. Whole Hearts.* and conversations about the aforementioned concepts (such as psychological safety) becoming increasingly common, we are quickly realizing that the most effective leaders are not only aware of the concept of bringing one's whole self to work, but welcome and know how to navigate and respond to this, including and especially when it is messy.

5. Help Your People Rediscover Their Inherent Resilience

Every single person has a reservoir of resilience within them. We have all had to learn how to navigate our bodies, language and the world around us. Each of us has failed in thousands of endeavors, over and over again. Sadly, a lot of this happened during a time in our lives that we cannot remember: childhood. A lot of us have consequently forgotten how resilient we are. Luckily, there is a much-needed conversation happening at the moment about resilience. Thought leaders such as Brené Brown are providing much-needed education on what constitutes resilience and why it matters.

Bringing resilience into the conversation in team meetings, check-ins, away days and performance reviews can help create a culture that supports your people to be comfortable with thinking and talking about resilience. Get to know your people—notice when they are depleted, in need of a recharge, dancing on the edge of burnout, or out of touch with their inherent resilience. This, again, requires a level of emotional intelligence and willingness to talk about emotional and psychological well-being, which can be intimidating and even uncomfortable at work, but the results are worth it: staff who can be more honest about what is really happening for them, who pay attention to their well-being and take action when they notice warning signs. Prevention is better than a cure.

6. Focus on Feedback

A Deliberately Developmental Leader understands the powerful role feedback plays in developing people and driving a business forward. Despite the prevalence of feedback in the many online spaces we inhabit—Amazon, Airbnb, Etsy, Trip Advisor and the like—most of us, if we are honest, are not huge fans of feedback. We do not particularly like giving it, and we bristle and brace ourselves inwardly when we receive it. We know it is valuable, but in most workplaces, feedback is typically just incorporated into quarterly, half-yearly, or annual intervals, only given or asked for during performance reviews or leadership 360s.

This does not mean that we are short on opinions. Quite the contrary. Many of us are quick to tell others exactly what is bothering us about the people we work with, but something happens when the person in question is in front of us. We instinctively balk, sugarcoat, soften or outright hide our opinions and thoughts from the person those thoughts are about. It is in many ways an entirely human thing to do: generally, people do not revel in the possibility of upsetting others or hurting their feelings by telling them about the things they did not do well or could have done better, or about the negative consequences of their decisions and actions, which can be painful to stomach.

This does not apply to everyone; on the contrary, many people are known for being extremely sharp-tongued, direct and blunt. While this can be refreshing—you pretty much always know where you stand with someone like this because you know that if they have something to say to you, they will say it—it can nevertheless leave people walking on metaphorical eggshells, especially if the feedback is given in an unstructured, aggressive or erratic way. There is a big difference between giving feedback for the purposes of supporting a colleague to grow or for the purpose of lashing out. Not knowing if you are going to be the target of criticism can erode psychological safety and may even create an anxiety-fueled, decidedly unsafe climate in a team or organization.

Deliberately Developmental Leaders know that giving feedback is an inherent and inescapable part of leadership. They know feedback is a central ingredient in providing effective mentorship, and that it is also vital in facilitating innovation, productivity and progress. DDLs think deeply about feedback and how to effectively incorporate it within the teams, departments or organizations they lead. They are conscious of the need to balance considering their colleagues' unique personalities and the ways in which they can most effectively receive feedback with making sure they are not protecting their feelings by not giving feedback, while at the same time not lashing out under the guise of giving feedback where it is needed. Intelligently incorporating feedback as a practice requires thought and reflective practice: trying something, reflecting on what works and iterating.

Getting to know people well enough to know what is effective and useful is usually a vital part of building a feedback culture. Build feedback into your structures so that it is part of the fabric of how the team functions. A lot of the empirical evidence I have reviewed from companies that explicitly incorporate feedback into their day-to-day functioning shows that although people find it psychologically tough—having your weakness highlighted and talked about out in the open can be challenging—they also find it incredibly refreshing and ultimately rewarding. There is a huge sense of relief that comes from knowing that people are not hiding their thoughts about you. Transparency helps foster psychological safety and in turn psychological safety allows for greater levels of honesty.

Leaders who take feedback seriously also need to be open to receiving it, from above, below and within; in practice, that means you might have to proactively seek out feedback from your seniors, from those you lead, and from yourself through self-reflection (coaching can provide a productive space in which to do this). As a leader, you set the precedent, which means you might have to confront any resistance you feel to receiving feedback.

A culture characterized by the presence of a lot of feedback tackles people's development areas with more gusto. When weaknesses are pointed out as the norm rather than the exception then the business stops investing energy into what Kegan and Laskow call the "second job no one is paying for"—the job of covering up, hiding and faking our way through the day.

In a Deliberately Developmental Organization the whole business would ideally be engaged in practices designed to foster personal growth alongside the pursuit of the business's priorities and tasks. Even if the rest of the organization you work in avoids the challenging yet rewarding work of being rigorous about self-development, as a leader you can still develop practices that encourage transparency with the team you lead.

The low levels of disengagement[17] in workplaces globally are in part because too many organizations ask people to work in challenging, stressful, high-pressure environments—often with little-to-no letup—without the crucial ingredient of personal growth. Adopting a deliberately developmental mentality and approach can help transform these conditions into an incubator for growth rather than a prescription for burnout. That alone is a compelling reason to explore becoming a Deliberately Developmental Leader.

Further Reading

Chapter 2: The Outcome of a Well-Defined Culture

1. Soundstripe culture deck
   https://www.slideshare.net/TravisTerrell2/soundstripe-culture-deck-2017

2. *Culture Decks Decoded* download
   https://www.culturegene.ai/books/culture-decks-decoded

Chapter 4: People Funnel

3. Glassdoor survey
   https://hbr.org/2017/01/what-matters-more-to-your-workforce-than-money

4. SalesLoft Careers Site
   https://salesloft.com/company/careers/

5. Runway East Culture Deck
   https://docsend.com/view/cwg89hf

Chapter 6: Onboarding, Probation, Performance Evaluation and Exit

6. Simon Sinek's TED Talk
   https://www.ted.com/talks/simon_sinek_how_great_leaders_inspire_action?language=en

Chapter 8: How to Embed Company Culture

7. DISC Profile Psychometric Tool
   https://www.discprofile.com/what-is-disc/overview/

Chapter 10: Trust, Transparency and Psychological Safety

8. Project Aristotle
https://rework.withgoogle.com/print/guides/57213126
55835136/

Chapter 11: Diversity and Inclusion

9. McKinsey "Delivering Through Diversity" report
https://www.mckinsey.com/~/media/mckinsey/busine
ss%20functions/organization/our%20insights/delivering
%20through%20diversity/delivering-through-
diversity_full-report.ashx

Chapter 12: Remote and Hybrid Work Environments

10. Buffer 4-day work week
https://open.buffer.com/4-day-workweek/

11. Andreas Klinger interview
https://www.culturegene.ai/post/cracking-the-code-of-
remote-working-lessons-from-the-future-of-work

12. Survey: How 165 startups are adapting to work from
home
https://www.forbes.com/sites/brettonputter/2020/04/1
3/how-165-startups-are-adapting-to-work-from-home-
culturegene/#55d902c765d6

13. Gitlab Single Source of Truth
https://about.gitlab.com/handbook/values/#single-
source-of-truth

14. Hotjar Team Manual
https://hotjar.atlassian.net/wiki/spaces/REC/pages/15
8040197/Core+Hours+Weekly+Structure

15. Muriel Maignan Wilkins for the Harvard Business Review
https://hbr.org/2014/11/signs-that-youre-a-micromanager

16. Paul J. Zak for the Harvard Business Review
https://hbr.org/2017/01/the-neuroscience-of-trust

Afterword
17. Gallup Employee Engagement
https://www.gallup.com/workplace/229424/employee-engagement.aspx